Organic Crafts

Organic Crafts

75 Earth-Friendly Art Activities

Kimberly Monaghan

CHICAGO
REVIEW
PRESS

Library of Congress Cataloging-in-Publication Data
Monaghan, Kimberly.
   Organic crafts : earth-friendly art activities / Kimberly
Monaghan.
      p. cm.
   Includes bibliographical references and index.
   ISBN-13: 978-1-55652-640-4
   ISBN-10: 1-55652-640-7
1. Handicraft—Juvenile literature. 2. Nature crafts—Juvenile
literature. I. Title.

TT160.M554 2007
745.5—dc22   2006031659

Cover design: Monica Baziuk
Cover illustration: Betsy Kulak
Interior design: Rattray Design
Interior illustration: Gail Rattray

Published by Chicago Review Press, Incorporated
814 North Franklin Street
Chicago, Illinois 60610
ISBN-13: 978-1-55652-640-4
ISBN-10: 1-55652-640-7
Printed in the United States of America
8 7 6 5

This book is dedicated to my two "bookends,"

who have supported me in all my ventures.

Thank you, Mike and Barbara, for all your love.

Why Can't We Pick Flowers in National Parks?

National and State park areas are set aside to preserve the scenery and the natural and historic objects for the enjoyment of all visitors. Everything in the park is protected by law. Do not pick flowers, collect rocks, take pine cones, or touch rock formations. When hiking, stay on the marked trails. This will keep these protected areas thriving for all to enjoy.

Contents

Acknowledgments

I owe a debt of gratitude to Cynthia Sherry, Lisa Rosenthal, and the entire team at Chicago Review Press. I truly appreciate Cynthia's patience in teaching me the ropes and Lisa's talent for listening, motivating, and making the editing process so much fun! My sincere appreciation also goes to MaryAnn Kohl with Bright Ring Publishing for encouraging me and helping me to get my manuscript into the right hands. Much love to my motivators, Colleen, Ruth, Eileen, Lisa Marie, Marge, Carol, Marley, Dorene, Pam, Lisa, and Judy of the Vernon Area Public Library Youth Services Department, who agreed to patiently test-run my projects and listen to never-ending stories. A spe-cial thanks to my writing partner, Sue Pinkowski, for many creative lunches. Sincere thanks also goes to Sandy Kamen Wisnewski and Esther Hershen-horn for their wonderful coaching, guidance, and encouragement. Thanks to Amanda, Anna, Emily, and Sarah for constructing all my crafts in a bag. And, of course, I couldn't forget those who intro-duced me to the natural world and all that it has to offer: Mom for the botany lessons; Dad for the spot-ting, casting, and berry-picking adventures; Tim and Skippy for all the intense nature hikes; Kathy for showing me what a freshwater eel looks like up close; and Mike for all his expertise, encourage-ment, and love.

An Introduction for Teachers, Parents, and Kids

For Teachers and Parents

Organic Crafts walks children through the woods, along the beach, and into grassy meadows to explore our natural surroundings. Everything around us has artistic beauty and a functional purpose, and this book invites children to take a closer look at the elements of nature. By exploring tiny pieces of our earth, from forest to seashore, we can better understand how nature works, how it enhances our lives, and learn to appreciate its beauty. Along the way children will discover imaginative ways to turn the ordinary into the extraord-

nary by making art from nature. They will learn to make creative use of natural and reusable resources, while exploring the many ways that nature is part of our lives, and about how important it is to preserve these essential resources.

Activities are divided into chapters that focus on key elements of nature, such as "Plants, Grasses, and Seeds" (chapter 4) and "Animals, Birds, and Insects" (chapter 5). This organization makes it ideal for structuring lesson plans that explore the world around us. When learning about our natural world, or any new topic, breaking the subject into manageable sections invites easier understanding and lasting comprehension. Just as *Organic Crafts* is laid out into six different components of the natural world, lessons can be designed as six phases, so that neither the child nor the teacher is overwhelmed. Instead a slower and more entertaining approach will provide ample opportunity for further exploration, research, and creativity. *Organic Crafts* is designed for the parent, teacher, or caregiver to use as a resource for creative playtime or classroom learning. It is also a resource for older readers to independently explore the natural world, learning how things work, and how nature creates amazing beauty. For example, when growing a Wildlife Seedling Tray in chapter 5, children of all ages will learn about the feeding cycles of wildlife and what types of plants promote the well-being of wildlife and enhance nature's life cycle. This knowledge may not only inspire budding botanists and horticulturists, but also may encourage viewing a plant as more than a mere thing of beauty, rather one of purpose. A handy "Teacher's Guide" in the back of the book will help with lesson planning, too.

Sometimes we begin a craft project without thinking about the materials we need or natural alternatives that are available. *Organic Crafts* provides a number of alternative earth-friendly materials (see pages xiv–xv for alternative recipes for homemade glue and paste that can be substituted whenever store-bought craft glue or paste is listed in the materials list) to complete craft activities and teaches children important lessons, such as the importance of recycling. Some crafts call for store-bought ingredients, such as wiggle eyes or florist's foam balls. These materials don't always have to be used. Invite kids to use their creativity in substituting readily available materials—small buttons instead of wiggle eyes and crumpled-up newspaper balls for the florist's foam balls—for store-bought ones. In addition, some crafts call for the use of glitter. This is always optional. Consider using tiny pieces of aluminum foil or confetti-sized pieces of colorful construction paper to make a picture sparkle.

Organic Crafts invites young children to explore fun ways to learn about, enjoy, and respect nature, and guides them in new ways to experience their surroundings. While doing the activities in this book, it is important to stress that each craft is a work of art and therefore, there is no *right* way to do each activity, and no two should be the same. After all, elementary exploration of the importance of our earth comes through artistic imagination. Most important, *Organic Crafts* teaches respect for our natural resources to encourage children to work (or play) to preserve our natural environment.

Nature Notes, added throughout the book, offer more fun-filled facts about the environment, people, places, and things—such as the mysterious rock formation known as Stonehenge—as well as ideas for further environmental exploration. Each chapter concludes with an Earth Action that presents great ideas and resources to address current challenges to our environment, such as the erosion of beaches, and how children can help preserve these important natural resources.

For Kids

Organic Crafts is your guide to having fun in the great outdoors, and you'll learn new ways to look at nature by turning things that come from the earth into a work of art! The art you create will give you and your friends a chance to discover nature and learn ways to help care for our environment, too. The environment is all the things in nature, living and nonliving, that surround us—everything, including us—so it's really important.

Although art is fun to look at and make, art can also be functional. *Functional* means that it's something that you can use, such as a vase, birdhouse, or a game. Don't worry if you don't have all the craft and natural materials needed for an activity. You can use your imagination to find other materials or supplies and make your artwork that much more unique. In chapter 6, "Reduce, Reuse, and Recycle," you'll learn many ways to reuse leftover materials to create new and beautiful works of art.

Have you ever been asked to bring your sneakers to art class? Probably not. But with *Organic Crafts*, sneakers are a must! Walking around and seeing the sights of nature is a big part of what we do as earth explorers and how we grow into nature artists. Most of the stuff you'll use in your art will come from nature. You'll need to take walks to collect the raw materials you'll need for these activities, such as leaves, twigs, stones, and seashells.

Let's begin with three important recipes. A *recipe* is a set of directions that tells you how to make one big thing out of a lot of smaller things. One of our recipes is for homemade Natural Glue, one is for homemade Natural Paste, and one is for natural paint made from cornstarch. These can be used in place of store-bought glue, paste, and paint and will make your nature crafts that much more organic. So whenever you see a recipe that calls for craft glue, paste, or paint, you can try these natural alternatives, too.

Before you begin any activity, gather all the smaller things, called ingredients, together in one place, and find a place where it's OK to work (ask an adult) *before* you start to follow the directions.

Natural Glue

Measuring cup
1/2 cup skim milk
Measuring spoons
2 tablespoons white vinegar
Spoon
Short drinking glass
3 paper towels
Rubber band
2 teaspoons water
1 teaspoon baking soda

1. Pour 1/2 cup of skim milk into the measuring cup.
2. Add 2 tablespoons of white vinegar. Mix well with the spoon.
3. Let the mixture stand for 5 minutes.
4. While you are waiting, take one paper towel and cover the open end of the short drinking glass.
5. Push down just a little on the center of the paper towel to create a small paper towel bowl inside the glass. Put the rubber band around the glass. This will keep the paper towel in place with the little bowl-shaped dimple still in the center of the paper towel.
6. After 5 minutes, pour the milk and vinegar mixture through the paper towel into the drinking glass.
7. Let this sit for about 1 hour. All the water will empty out of the mixture into the glass.
8. After the hour is over, use the spoon to scrape up the dried mixture that is left on top of the paper towel.
9. Gently press this dried mixture between the two clean paper towels. Make sure to squeeze out all the extra water. It is very important to squeeze out all the extra water, so you may want to let the mixture sit for a few minutes until the water dries up.
11. Scrape off this dried mixture and place it back into the measuring cup. Add 2 teaspoons of water and 1 teaspoon of baking soda.
12. Mix well. Your Natural Glue is now ready to use. You will only need to use a little bit of this glue for your paper projects because it is very thick and very strong. But your Natural Glue will take longer to dry than store-bought glue.

Natural Paste

Adult supervision required

Measuring cup
$\frac{1}{4}$ cup cold water
Saucepan
$\frac{1}{2}$ cup flour
Spoon

1. Pour the cold water into the saucepan. Slowly add the flour into it while stirring.
2. Mix well with the spoon, getting rid of any lumps.
3. With the help of an adult, put saucepan on the stove and heat on low. Slowly stir mixture as it heats until it is a thick paste. This takes about 20 minutes.
4. Let it cool. Now you can use this in place of store-bought paste.

Cornstarch Paint

Adult supervision required

Cup for mixing
Measuring spoons
Measuring cups
1 tablespoon cold water
2 tablespoons cornstarch
Spoon
1 cup very hot tap water or boiling water
Food coloring, different colors

1. Put cold water into the cup. Add in the cornstarch and mix.
2. Stir until mixture is smooth and all lumps are gone.
3. With the help of an adult, slowly add the cup of hot water while mixing. Stir again until smooth.
4. Choose the color you want to make your Cornstarch Paint. Add two or three drops of this food coloring and mix thoroughly.

You can also store this paint in an airtight container, such as a baby food jar, for later use. Remember, you can always add more water if it gets dry.

You can also make paint from some vegetables and fruits. See page 70 for a paint recipe from crushed fruit or vegetables.

When you do *Organic Crafts* you will need tools and supplies. You should collect these and put them in an Earth Art Box so that they'll be ready for fun whenever you want them.

Safety Tips

Here are some safety tips that will help make your time exploring the earth a fun and safe time.

1. Read the directions fully at least one time before you begin.
2. If you have questions, ask an adult to help. Don't be afraid to ask. Remember that working together can make a project more fun!
3. Some crafts require the help of an adult. But *always* make sure that an adult is nearby in case you need help or have questions.
4. Many of these art projects call for the use of glue. It is best to cover a worktable with an old newspaper or a cloth that can be recycled later before using glue or paint so that you do not damage furniture.
5. Work outside or in a room with windows or a fan when you are using glue and rubber cement. This will help move the air around and keep it safe and fresh.
6. Some projects require you to dig for things. Always ask permission from the adult in charge before digging, even in your own backyard. Sometimes electric wires or cables have been buried nearby, which can cause harm to you when they are touched.
7. Some plants and trees are not friendly and may be poisonous. Be sure that you know what type of plants, trees, and bushes they are before touching them. Also be careful with creatures you find in the wild. Protect yourself by asking an adult to help you find out about all the things you see before you touch. As beautiful as our earth is, it has many ways of protecting itself. Be safe, and teach yourself before you reach!

Earth Art Box

The Earth Art Box is the special place where you keep all the tools you need to explore the world around you. It's also a great place to store the pretty and interesting things you find during your nature walks. That way you'll have them ready for a later project.

- Old shoebox or cardboard box small enough for you to carry but big enough to store tools and art and craft supplies
- Cloth or plastic bag with handles for collecting things
- Pencil or pen
- Notebook or nature journal to make notes or write down ideas when you are walking in nature (You will learn how to make a nature journal in chapter 1.)
- Rubber or gardening gloves (These will come in handy when you are collecting materials and will also help protect your hands when you are making crafts.)
- 1-inch-wide paintbrush to use for dusting off rocks and cleaning up other interesting things you find outside (You can also clean your paint-

brush in an old coffee can filled with water and reuse your brush for new craft projects.)

🐦 Ruler to help you measure things for your projects and also to draw straight lines

🐦 Metal spoon or gardener's trowel, which is like a small shovel, to dig up materials from the ground

🐦 A few jars or containers with lids for the dirt, sand, or clay that will be used in your crafts

Here are some of the things you may find outside during your nature walks. These can be saved for a later project.

Pinecones	Grasses
Seashells	Bark
Rocks	Twigs
Pebbles	Leaves

1
Trees, Leaves, and Twigs

Trees are a very important part of our world. Trees give humans and animals what we need most to live—*oxygen*! Humans breathe in oxygen every time they take a breath, and then our bodies turn it into *carbon dioxide*, which we breathe out. Oxygen is what we need for our cells, organs, and bodies to function properly so we can be healthy. Where does the oxygen that we need to live come from? It comes from trees. Through the magic of nature, the leaves of trees take in carbon dioxide that we breathe out and turn it into oxygen, which goes back into the air for us to breathe in. Already you can see why trees are so important. But trees also provide food, shelter, and shade from the sun for squirrels, koalas, woodpeckers, owls, monkeys, and many other animals as well as humans. Stuff people use every day is made from lumber that comes from trees, including houses, boats, and big-league baseball bats. Newspapers and books are printed on paper made from trees. Rubber and maple syrup come from the soft inner layer of the tree, just under the bark. The bark of a tree is also turned into products, such as cork and different kinds of medicines, such as aspirin, slippery elm, tea tree, and quinine (used to treat malaria). Budding from the twigs of the tree are the nuts and fruits that we enjoy eating. We are also able to get fuel by burning the wood scraps from a tree, some of which are turned into steam to make power.

It would be hard to imagine life without the products made from trees. But trees are being cut down and forests are disappearing faster than new ones can be planted. The process of clearing or cutting down the trees in our forests is called *deforestation*, and it's unhealthy for our environment. Organizations like the Sierra Club help to protect trees and to teach people about the importance of caring for and planting new trees. You can help, too. Along with planting new trees, you can stop more from being cut down by reusing stuff made from trees. Scrap pieces of wood, old newspaper, and used paper that will be thrown away can be reused for new craft or school projects. (You'll learn about the importance of recycling in the final chapter.) For the protection of living trees, whenever you need bark, twigs, and leaves for an *Organic Crafts* project, please collect what you need from the ground.

Tree Talker

Ages 6 and under

There are so many different types of trees. If you took a walk in your neighborhood or a nearby park, you could probably find at least 10 different types of trees. You also might see very different types of plants that are really trees in disguise. Did you know that the twisting trunks of the mountaintop bristlecones out west and the spiny boojum shooting out of the desert are trees? Trees come in all shapes and sizes and can be found everywhere in the world. Sometimes it just takes a little bit of investigating to see if that funny-looking plant is really just a tree in disguise. Some trees, such as the oak, are friendly. They have strong branches that you can hang a tire swing from and thick trunks in which squirrels can make a nest. Some trees are not as friendly. Poison sumac can look a lot like a small shrub or a tree, but is dangerous to humans, causing a painful rash.

A great way to learn about types of trees and to teach others about trees is to make a Tree Talker.

Materials

Leaves, needles, bark, and/or seeds from different trees, different sizes

Tree identification (naming) book*

1 package 3 × 5-inch unlined index cards or paper cut the same size

Black marker

1 sheet poster board, 18 × 24 inches

5 sheets different-colored tissue paper

Small cup for mixing glue

Craft glue or homemade Natural Glue, p. xiv

1 cup water

1½- or 1-inch paintbrush

*Cassie, Brian. *National Audubon Society First Field Guide: Trees.* New York: Scholastic, 1999.

1. Sort the leaves, needles, bark, and/or seeds you've collected into different piles so that all the items from the same tree are together. Use a tree identification book to make sure that you have the correct name of the tree for each collection pile.

2. Take an index card and turn it so that the short sides are on the top and bottom. Fold the index card in half. Write the name of the tree inside the card for each of your collection piles.

3. Place the poster board flat on a table or work surface.

4. Tear your colored tissue into large strips about 1 inch wide and any length from 6 to 12 inches.

5. Put 7 tablespoons of glue into your mixing cup. Add 1 teaspoon of water so that the glue becomes a thin mixture. Using the paint brush spread some of the glue mixture on your poster board

6. Place your torn tissue strips on top of the glue in every direction. Sometimes overlap them (to make a new color) and sometimes not, to make a colorful background for your board. Using your paintbrush dipped in the glue mixture, lightly coat the top of the tissue so that your tissue design will stay put. The board does not need to be covered completely. Leave spaces between each strip of tissue paper. Just make sure to place your tissue paper in a design you like.

7. Let your board dry completely.

8. After your board is dry, lay out your collection piles with their tree-title index card on the board.

9. Using the glue from the bottle, stick each piece from each tree collection to the board next to the correct tree-title index card. Glue down the back of the folded tree-title index card so that it can be opened up to show the name of the tree. Leave enough space between your cards and collections so that it's clear which collections belong with which card.

10. When your board is completely dry, you can play guessing games with your friends, your family, your classmates, and your teacher about the types of trees that grow where you live!

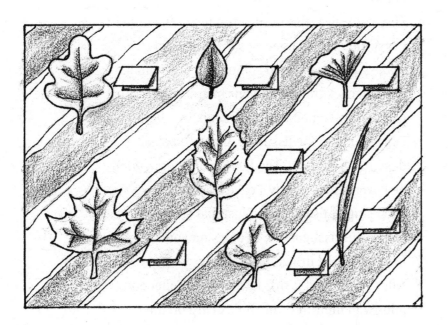

Homemade Paper

Ages 7 and up

The word *paper* comes to us from the Latin word *papyrus*. Papyrus is a reed, or tall thick grass, that grows in the Nile River valley in Egypt. Thousands of years ago, the Egyptian people needed something to write on. They crushed and pressed the papyrus reeds. Then they pasted the pressed reeds together to make a strong sheet several layers thick. This produced a very heavy form of paper. Like the Egyptians, you can make your own Homemade Paper using grasses, lint from your dryer, and old scraps of waste paper.

Adult supervision required

Materials

1 sheet newspaper

2 sheets paper, such as office, construction, or scrap paper, 8½ × 11 inches

1 measuring cup that will hold at least 2 cups liquid

¼ cup dryer lint

¼ cup crumbled or shaved tree bark and broken up
 twigs (optional)

¼ cup leaves

Blender

2 cups water

Wooden spoon

1 handful small flower petals and grass blades

1 12 × 12–inch piece of an old window screen with
 very small openings

Rectangular plastic tub, at least 9 × 11 inches

Can of nonstick cooking spray

1. Take the old papers and newspaper and shred
 them into very tiny pieces. Put the shredded
 paper into a measuring cup, filling it about
 three-quarters full.

2. Fill the measuring cup completely by adding
 some of the dryer lint, tree bark, leaves, and
 grass. Put this mixture into a blender along with
 1 cup of water.

3. Blend on low until all the paper is finely shredded and you have a thick mixture that looks a lot
 like paste. You should be able to stir it with a
 wooden spoon. If your mixture is too thick to stir
 with the wooden spoon, *slowly* add a little more
 water until the mixture is smooth.

🐦 *Nature Notes*

Plentiful Paper?

Have you ever wondered what happens to a piece of paper that is tossed into the waste-basket? No matter how much paper we throw away, there always seems to be more paper ready when we want to write, color, or paint. This is true today, but how long will the end-less supply of paper last?

Did you know that it takes many trees just to print a year's worth of newspapers? In just one month, 1.7 million copies of the *New York Times* Sunday edition are printed. Each Sunday *Times* has hundreds of pages. Can you imagine how many trees it takes to print that many newspapers? Paper makes up one of the biggest parts of our garbage—more than plas-tic, glass, and metals. Many people do not real-ize that much of the paper we use can be recycled. *Recycling* means turning materials into new things. If we collect our paper waste for recycling, we can help to save our forests and stop garbage from taking the place of nature in our world. (In chapter 6, you will learn about more ways to turn waste into things you can use again.)

Nature Notes

John James Audubon

In 1803 John James Audubon (1785–1851) came to America when he was a young man. His father wanted him to become a businessperson, but John liked to draw and paint. He loved to spend his time in the woods studying animals and plants and drawing their pictures in his journals. He decided to spend the rest of his life studying and drawing, and he became one of the best-known nature artists ever. His paintings of North American birds can be found in many museums today, and his books, filled with his beautiful drawings of birds and animals, continue to be sold all over the world.

4. Add your flower petals but do not turn on the blender. Instead use your wooden spoon to stir your flower petals into your paper mixture. Mixing them thoroughly will help make them part of the mixture and more securely attached to the paper.
5. Place your window screen flat on top of the plastic tub. Spray it lightly with the nonstick cooking spray.
6. Carefully spread your paper mixture on top of the screen with the wooden spoon. The tub below the screen will catch all the extra water as your paper mixture dries.
7. Allow your paper to dry completely. This may take a day or two.
8. When it is all dry, peel your Homemade Paper from the screen and use it to write on.

Family Tree

Ages 6 and under

A family tree can be used to learn about our family or to tell others about it. A family tree can be a drawing of lines and circles showing who the members of a family are and how they are related. Or it can be a picture of a tree where you write names of the members of your family on the branches. From our sisters and brothers to our mother and father, and our grandparents and our grandparents' parents, family trees are fun ways to learn about who we are and where we come from. With just a few leaves and twigs you can make your own Family Tree.

Materials

1 piece scrap paper, 8 × 12 inches
Pencil
1 sheet construction paper or poster board, 24 × 36 inches
1 long twig, 12 inches long
10–15 twigs, 2–5 inches long
Wood glue for twigs
Craft glue or homemade Natural Glue, p. xiv
Heavy book, such as a telephone book or dictionary
20 or more large leaves
1 sheet construction paper, 8½ × 11 inches, different color from the larger one
Black marker
Scissors

1. Make a list of names to include on your Family Tree. The list should include your brothers, sisters, mother, father, and grandparents. Don't forget to include yourself. You may also want to include your cousins, aunts, uncles, and anyone else who is part of your family.

2. Draw a practice sketch of your Family Tree. Planning how your Family Tree will look will make doing your craft easier. Start by drawing the trunk of a tree and several branches, using your pencil and the scrap piece of paper. Write your name on the trunk of the tree along with any brothers and sisters you may have. Above those names write your mother and father's names, and above them those of your grandparents. Add any other names you wish. Just make sure that your father's family is on one side of the tree and your mother's on another. But remember that your Family Tree is your own design and can be designed any way

you wish. This sketch will guide you when you are making your craft.

3. Place the large sheet of construction paper flat on a table or work surface.

4. Put your twigs on top of the paper in the shape of a tree. The biggest twig, the one measuring about 12 inches long, should be placed vertically on the paper, like a tree trunk. The remaining twigs can be placed on either side of the large twig, shooting out, just like tree branches.

5. When you are happy with the way your tree looks, carefully pick up each twig, one at a time. Squirt a little bit of the wood glue on the underside of the twig and then place it firmly back onto your paper. Do this for each twig until your tree has been glued firmly in place. Carefully place a large, heavy book, such as a telephone book or dictionary, on top of the twigs. Let your work dry.

6. Now you will need to add leaves to your tree. Just as with the twigs, place the leaves on the paper first to decide which branch they will be connected to. Do this until they are all where you want them. Some can be placed above and some below each branch. But remember, this is your

own work of art; you can make your tree look any way you like.

7. Put a few drops of glue on the back of each leaf and press it firmly in place. Again, do this one at a time to protect your design.

8. Finally, add the names to your Family Tree. On the second piece of colored construction paper, use the marker to write down the names of the members of your family. Begin with your name and then the names of any brothers or sisters you may have. Next, write down your parents' names, those of your aunts and uncles, those of cousins and grandparents. After you have written down as many names as you know, you may want to ask your parents to help you with more names, such as those of great-grandparents and great-aunts and -uncles. You can make your Family Tree as big or as small as you like.

9. When all the names have been written down, carefully cut each one out.

10. Now place each name on the tree where it belongs. You may want to start with your name somewhere near the trunk of your tree and your brothers and sisters nearby. Put your parents' names above yours, and your

grandparents' names above them. As babies are born and people marry, new people become part of your family. You may want to save some paper to add those names when the time comes. Your names may be placed on top of leaves, twigs, or on the background paper. The more you overlap items, the more your Family Tree is an artistic collage.

11. When you have placed the names where you want, use the glue to stick them to the paper.

12. Once your picture has dried completely, you can hang it up in your room or in a special place where everyone can admire your growing Family Tree.

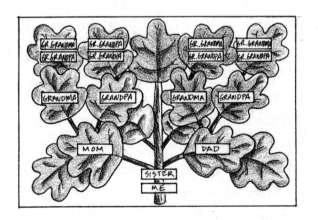

Nature Journal

Ages 6 and under

A journal is a book in which you write your secret thoughts, record all your fun adventures, and draw pictures of things you see. A journal can also be used to record, or set down in writing, things you've learned or discovered. John James Audubon used a journal to record notes and draw pictures of the birds of North America. Wilderness explorers Meriwether Lewis (1774–1809) and William Clark (1770–1838) used journals to record what they saw on their journeys out west in 1804–1806. Many things we've learned about history and our natural world come from historical journals. Maybe someday the Nature Journal you make will become an important piece of natural history!

Materials

5–10 sheets 8½ × 11-inch paper or Homemade Paper (see activity on p. 4)

🐦 *Nature Notes*

Arbor Day

Julius Sterling Morton (1832–1902) knew how important trees were to protect farms from storms and blizzards, and for providing food and shelter to all living creatures. In 1872 Mr. Morton created Arbor Day to educate people about the important role trees play in our lives. *Arbor* is a Latin word for tree. In April each state decides what day it will declare Arbor Day—a day for planting and taking care of trees! To find out when Arbor Day is celebrated in your state, go to www.arbor-day.net.

2 pieces cardboard, 8½ × 5 inches or larger

Scissors

Hole puncher

Pencil

3 or more colorful leaves

Marker or pen

Craft glue or homemade Natural Glue, p. xiv

Plastic cup

¼ cup water

2-inch-wide paintbrush

Spoon

2 strands twine or ribbon, 12 inches long

1. Fold each sheet of paper in half, lengthwise. Cut each sheet of paper in half along this fold line so that the paper size is roughly 8½ × 5 inches. These pieces of paper will be the inside of your journal. Your cutting doesn't have to be exact or neat. In fact, the rougher the edges, the more artistic your journal will look.

2. Cut the two pieces of cardboard down to roughly the same size as your paper. These will be the front and back covers of your journal, so make sure they are big enough to cover the pages.

3. Use your hole puncher to make two sets of holes through your front and back covers along one of

the longer sides of your cardboard, one set of holes nearer the top, one set nearer the bottom.

4. Take several sheets of your paper and line them up underneath one of the cardboard cover pieces. Use a pencil to mark a dot for where you should use the hole puncher.

5. Use the pencil marks to line up the inside pages of your journal and use the hole puncher. Line up the two pieces of cardboard, and put the front cover with the holes atop the cardboard for the back cover.

6. Write your name and the title for your journal on the front cover piece of cardboard.

7. Squeeze two or three drops of glue on the back of your colorful leaves. Put the leaves on the cover of your journal to decorate around the title. Pour a spoonful of glue into your plastic cup and add a few drops of water. Mix it thoroughly with your paintbrush until it looks like paint. You may have to add a little more water to get the mixture smooth. Add it slowly. Using your paintbrush, paint a thin layer of glue over the top of the leaves to cover. This will not only make your leaves stick to the front of your journal, but also will give the cover a strong, shiny coat. Let dry overnight.

8. Now it is time to assemble your journal. Place the back piece of cardboard down. Then stack the paper and the cover cardboard on top so that the punched holes line up.

9. Thread your twine or ribbon through the punched holes and tie a firm knot or bow. Trim the extra length of twine with your scissors.

You are now ready to write about your world in your homemade Nature Journal.

Twig Trivet

Ages 7 and up

Twigs and small branches that fall on the ground often clutter a garden or get in the way of lawnmowers. Many people spend hours picking up fallen twigs and branches to toss away or to use as fuel. Have you ever had the chore of helping to clean up the yard by picking up fallen twigs? These twigs and small branches from trees can be sturdy materials for many crafts.

Remember: in order not to hurt or injure living trees, bushes, or plants, it is important not to pull or cut branches directly from a tree but only to use the ones that have fallen to the ground. Some of the twigs that you find on the ground can be turned into a Twig Trivet to use in the kitchen or by a campfire.

Materials

20 small twigs, 6–8 inches long, with any branches taken off
Scissors
12 fabric strips, 24 inches long and no more than 3 inches wide (Fabric strips can be torn from old fabric, sheets, clothing, socks, or smaller scraps of fabric sewn or tied tightly together to make longer strips.)

1. Select 10 twigs and lay them next to one another on a flat surface. Starting on the left side of your group of twigs, take one strip of fabric. Gently weave it through the twigs, going over the top of one, then under the next, and repeating until done.
2. When you reach the right side of the twigs, weave the remaining strip of fabric back toward you. Tie a knot where the fabric ends meet. Be sure not to pull the woven fabric too tight. You want the twigs to lie flat against a table.
3. Take a second strip of fabric and weave it the same way through the right side of your twig group. Start from the left side, but this time weave to the right and back again to the left, and so on. Be sure to tie the two ends together when they meet on the left side.
4. With at least two more strips of fabric, weave through the center part of your twig group. Start with the first strip on the right side and the second strip on the left side of the twigs.

5. Do the same with the remaining twigs, creating two separate flat, woven twig groups.

6. Place one of the twig groups on top of the other. Using the remaining two fabric strips, weave both twig groups together by pulling the fabric up through both sets of twigs and down through both sets of twigs. Soon you'll have a thick sturdy group of twigs woven tightly together. It may be a little lumpy and not lie completely flat. That's OK, though, because over time and with use, your Twig Trivet will change as it protects tables and counters from hot pots, pans, and dishes.

Kindling Basket

Ages 6 and under

One of the best things about a cold winter or damp summer's day is being warmed by a toasty fire. You may have memories of sitting by the fireside with your friends or family sharing sledding stories and sipping hot chocolate. Or perhaps you have gone to a summer camp where there was a big bonfire for roasting marshmallows and hotdogs. Building a fire is a lot of work, and should always be left to an adult. One way you can help is by making a Kindling Basket! *Kindling* is a collection of materials called *biomass*. Forest biomass includes scraps of trees, such as twigs, leaves, and bark that are small and dry and will catch fire quickly and keep a fire burning. In this activity you will use raffia, a popular decorative fiber. (Natural raffia comes from the raffia palms in Madagascar, an island just off the southeastern coast of Africa.) It is often dyed in various colors.

Adult supervision required

Materials

Bag for collecting

6 strips raffia or twine, each 8 inches long

Scissors

1 bag store-bought potpourri, old, dried potpurri, or you can make your own potpourri (see recipe on p. 67)

1 paper lunch bag, or 2 bags if you'll make your own potpourri

Basket, any size

1. Take your bag for collecting materials for kindling on a nature hike. You will need to look for all sorts of materials that can be used for kindling. Kindling is just another name for small pieces of wood that are easy to burn and are used to start a fire. Look for fallen twigs, dried leaves, pinecones, or dried grasses, and put them in your bag.

2. When you return from your hike, separate your collection into piles of twigs, pinecones, grasses, and leaves.

3. Using the raffia or twine, tie the group of twigs into a bundle. Do the same for the grasses.

4. Put all the dry leaves into a paper lunch bag. Tie the top of it closed with a piece of raffia or twine.

5. If you made your own potpourri, you can put it into the second paper lunch bag and tie it with a piece of raffia or twine.

6. Put the bundles of twigs, grasses, the bag of leaves, the bag of potpourri, and all the pinecones into the basket. The twigs, grasses, and leaves will help start a fire. The pinecones and potpourri will make the fire pop with different colors. Remember to give your kindling basket to an adult so they can safely start a fire! The materials for your Kindling Basket can be found all year long. This means that you can make an awesome holiday gift even in the middle of win-

Nature's Vase

Ages 7 and up

As you have discovered, many of the arts and crafts in this book use tools you find on nature walks. Walking in nature is a great way to get exercise and fresh air. Nature walks can also be a source of great ideas for your own arts and crafts. When you take a walk through the woods, a park, or along sand dunes, take a look around at all the plants and animals. Look up at the sky and see the towering treetops. Look down at the sand and rough rocks. Close your eyes and smell the salty sea and fresh pine needles. Did you get any ideas for a picture you would like to draw or a craft you would like to create? It is possible to use everything you see and smell in your arts or crafts projects. Ordinary things that you already own, such as a pencil cup, a plastic vase, or a candle, can be turned into beautiful art with just a few things you collect from your nature walks. Once you understand how to put together things you find on your nature walks and other household objects, you can create and decorate with your own earth art, such as this Nature's Vase.

Materials

3 sheets newspaper
20 or more small twigs, 10 inches long; a longer branch can be broken up to make smaller twigs
Plastic vase, old plastic container, or plastic butter tub
Rubber cement
Wood glue
3 pieces raffia or a ribbon long enough to wrap around the plastic vase two times

1. Spread two sheets of newspaper on your work surface.
2. Rip a strip from one sheet of newspaper wide enough to cover the outside of your vase or plastic tub.
3. Break your twigs up so that they are the same height as the vase from top to bottom. The twigs do not need to be the exact length of the vase. Some may be a little longer or shorter.

Tree Skin

Just like people, trees, too, have skin! The skin that covers a tree is called bark. Just like our skin, bark has many tiny holes, or *pores*, to protect the tree inside from becoming too dry and also from disease and attacks by animals. It may be easy to peel the skin, or bark, from a tree, but it's bad for the trees. Remember when you skinned your knees? Besides, the best tree bark to use for arts and crafts is the bark that you find on the ground. Bark can be soaked in soapy water to remove any bugs or loose dirt. Then, let the bark dry completely in the sun before you use it.

4. Put rubber cement on the outside of the vase or plastic tub. Wrap the torn newspaper strip around it and let it dry.

5. Using the wood glue, stick the twig pieces on the newspaper-covered vase or tub. Repeat the gluing and sticking of twigs until the entire plastic vase or tub is covered.

6. Let the glue dry overnight. If a twig falls off the next day, put a little more glue on the vase and press the twig back in place.

7. When the glue is completely dry, wrap the raffia or ribbon around the vase once. Carefully tie it into a knot or a bow. Now your Nature's Vase is ready to hold flowers or a plant.

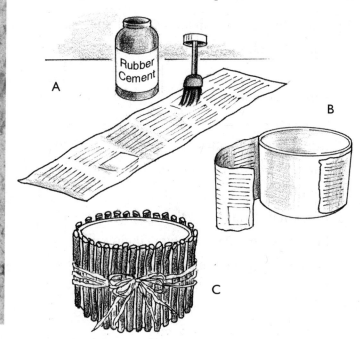

Skin Drums

Ages 6 and under

Drums make great music. Many handmade drums are beautiful works of art. Some drums are decorated with carvings, paint, beads, or unusual objects. Native Americans used animal skins to make drums. In this craft you will make a Skin Drum using a different kind of skin: earth-friendly tree bark.

Materials

1 piece construction paper, any size
Craft glue or homemade Natural Glue, p. xiv
Small oatmeal container
Scissors
1 bag dried beans
2 sheets waxed paper, 5 × 5 inches
1 thick rubber band
20 or more pieces of tree bark, enough to cover an
    8½ × 11–inch piece of paper
Wood glue
Crayons or paint and brush (optional)
2 brightly colored ribbons or raffia, 24 inches long

1. Glue the construction paper around the outside of the oatmeal container, using the craft glue. Trim any extra paper off the edges so that the container is nice and even. This will be the base of the drum.

2. Put a handful of dried beans inside the drum.

3. Tightly cover the opening on top with the two sheets of waxed paper. Wrap the rubber band around the waxed paper to hold it in place. You may need someone to help you hold the waxed paper in place while you put on the rubber band. Smooth out the paper and pull it tight against the opening.

4. Decorate your drum by attaching the tree bark to the construction paper using the wood glue. You should glue the bark in sections. Let each section dry before moving on to the next section, so that each section dries firmly and will not fall off when you are handling it. You do not have to cover the entire drum base with bark. You can fill in spaces with dried beans, color them with crayons or paint, or leave the spaces between the bark empty. You can decorate the drum in your own unique way.

5. Let your drum dry overnight.

6. Once the wood glue is completely dry, carefully wrap one ribbon around the top part of the

🍃 Nature Notes

Working Leaves

Leaves are hard at work every day helping a tree stay alive. A leaf may be pretty to look at and simple to draw, but it is actually a very complex part of a tree or plant. A leaf works hard to feed and protect trees and plants—a leaf protects a plant from losing too much water. Water is an important ingredient that helps trees and plants grow, and leaves take in sunlight and gases from the air for photosynthesis. *Photosynthesis* (FOE-toe-SIN-the-sis) is a chemical process in which a tree or plant creates energy to live. This energy fuels the tree or plant. It is also there for the insects, animals, and people who depend on plants for energy!

Want to learn more? Check out *Exploring the World of Leaves* by Raymond A. Wohlrabe. New York: Crowell, 1976.

drum. Tie it into a knot. Wrap the second ribbon around the bottom part of your drum. Tie it into a knot, too.

7. Tie both ends of the ribbons together so that you have a handle to carry your drum with or to hang it on a wall. Your Skin Drum is ready to shake, beat, and play with!

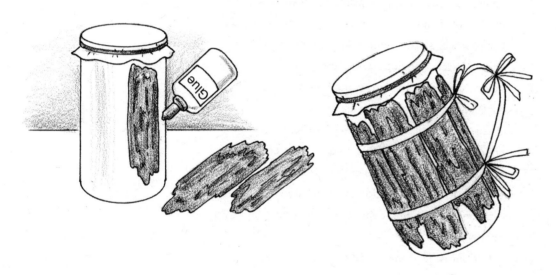

Bark Boat

Ages 7 and up

Tree bark was once very plentiful and is easy to bend and work with. Native Americans made canoes from bark along with skins and wood. Pioneers learned from the Native Americans. They used bark and wood to make boats to help them explore unknown waterways. This Bark Boat uses thin bark, such as that from willow or birch trees, to help keep the canoe light and able to float.

Adult supervision required

Materials

1 top of a Styrofoam egg carton

Scissors

3 small twigs, about 5 inches in length

20 thin pieces bark, enough to cover the sides of the egg carton

Rubber cement

1 8½ × 11–inch piece construction paper

Needle with a large eye

1 piece string, 10 inches long

1 twig, 6 inches long

1 piece thin rope or twine, 24 inches long

Craft glue or homemade Natural Glue, p. xiv

1 small piece modeling clay the size of the tip of your thumb or you can make your own salt clay (see page 99).

1. Use the scissors to cut six small holes on the sides of the egg carton top. The holes should be across from one another, three on one side and three on the other. The holes should be small, yet big enough to fit the ends of the twigs through.

2. Place each twig into the slits crosswise so that you will have three tiny benches in your canoe.

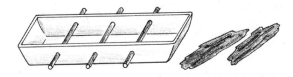

3. Cover the outside of your boat with rubber cement and stick bark on all sides. Let dry.

4. While the canoe is drying, cut a large triangle shape out of your construction paper. Starting from one corner of the paper, cut with your scissors in a diagonal to the bottom.

5. Thread your needle with the string. You may need an adult to help you to do this.

6. Poke the threaded needle through the corner of your paper. Sew upward in a straight stitch pattern of in and out, in and out along the flat part of the triangle. Leave several inches of thread on each end.

7. Tie the paper triangle to the top part of your twig like a sail on a ship. Tie the corner of the paper triangle to the other end of the twig.

8. Trim out your boat with the rope or twine. Place some craft glue around the top edge of your boat. Run the rope or twine along the top. Let dry.

9. Put the little bit of your modeling clay on the bottom end of the twig. Use your hand or the tabletop to press the bottom of the clay flat so that your sail will stand up.

10. Put some rubber cement on the bottom, flat part of the clay, and place it in the middle of your boat. Let all the glue and rubber cement dry well. When you are done, see whether your Bark Boat will float in your sink or in the bathtub.

Sparkling Sea Scene

Ages 6 and under

When trees drop their leaves in autumn, the red, yellow, or orange colors, and hand, heart, fruit, or fan shapes are pretty to look at. Leaves are much like snowflakes, because each one is different in size, texture, and color. Like clouds on a summer day, leaves can take the shape of many different things. One of the shapes you can make when you put a few leaves together is a fish swimming in the sparkling blue sea—a Sparkling Sea Scene.

Adult supervision required

Materials

2 10 × 10-inch sheets waxed paper

4 big leaves shaped like a pear, such as a leaf from an oak, hickory, ash, or mulberry tree

8 small leaves shaped like a pear

10 or more long blades of thin green grass

¼ cup tiny broken crayon pieces in orange, peach, and brown colors (these pieces should be no bigger than the tip of your pinky finger)

Tube of blue gel toothpaste

Toothpick

Tiny pieces aluminum foil or glitter (optional)

Small flower petals, various colors, or sequins (optional)

Thick towel

Iron

Ironing board

1. Lay one sheet of waxed paper on a table or work surface.
2. Place your four biggest leaves sideways on top of the waxed paper. These leaves will be the bodies of your fish.
3. Add the 8 smaller leaves by placing two at the back end of each of the fish bodies to be the fish fins.
4. Place the blades of grass along the bottom of your picture, standing up and down like wavy seaweed on the ocean floor.
5. Sprinkle the shaven or broken crayon pieces along the bottom of your picture in between the grass. (Once melted, these crayon pieces will become the coral reef in your sea scene.)

6. Using the toothpaste, carefully draw several very thin wavy lines above your fish in a upright direction (side to side). Use the toothpick to form the toothpaste lines into waves. You can also make bubbles coming from your fish's mouths. Be careful not to use too much toothpaste, because the toothpaste images will grow wider when you iron your picture flat.

7. Lightly sprinkle the aluminum foil around your sea scene. Place the flower petals around to decorate your sea scene. This will make your sea sparkle like the sun shining down on the water.

8. When you are happy with the way your picture looks, place the second sheet of waxed paper on top.

9. Now you will need the help of an adult. Have the adult move your picture to the ironing board and carefully lay a towel on top of the waxed paper.

10. The adult should turn the iron on to a low (warm) setting. Finally, the adult should run a warm iron over the towel until the two pieces of waxed paper melt together. When the adult is finished ironing and your work has cooled down, your Sparkling Sea Scene is complete. You can hang it on a wall or in the window where the sun's rays will make the sea sparkle

even more! Want more ideas for leaf shapes? Check out *Look What I Did with a Leaf!* by Morteza E. Sohi. New York: Walker, 1993.

Scented Leaf Basket

Ages 6 and under

Leaves have different textures at different times of the year. In the spring many leaves have a soft texture; they feel smooth and velvety and can easily bend. This is because the leaf is new and full of life. In midsummer and in autumn leaves begin to dry and have a brittle texture; they break apart easily. Dry leaves make healthy soil for new plants, because they easily crumble and can be quickly broken down and soaked back into the soil. This process of returning natural matter to the soil is called *decomposition*. It is how soil becomes full of nutrients to grow new things. For this craft you should use dried leaves that you find on the ground. Once you have created your Scented Leaf Basket, fill it with a little dirt and plant seeds to grow inside it. You can then plant the entire leaf basket outside in the ground. The best time to start this activity is midsummer or early autumn, when you start to find dried leaves on the ground. If you wait too long, you will not be able to plant your leafy basket outside if the weather becomes cold where you live.

Materials

Plastic bowl
1 lemon, cut in half
Spoon
Jar petroleum jelly
Bag full of large dried leaves, enough to coat the bowl with three layers of leaves (see below)
Craft glue or homemade Natural Glue, p. xiv
Paintbrush
Dirt
6 or more seeds that grow in the late summer and fall, such as American daisy, Texas bluebonnet, zinnia, prairie coneflower, and other wildflowers

1. Turn the plastic bowl upside down. Using the spoon, scoop out some of the petroleum jelly. Spread it on the flat side of the cut lemon.
2. Rub the lemon all over the bottom of the bowl. This adds scent and also keeps the leaves from sticking to the bowl.

3. Place leaves all over the bottom (and sides, if it has sides) of the bowl. Smooth them out.

4. With your paintbrush, spread some glue on top of the leaves. Squeeze some of the juice out of your lemon on top. Again, the lemon juice will make the basket smell good!

5. Add more leaves and smooth them out.

6. Add more glue with your paintbrush. Squeeze more lemon juice before adding a third layer of leaves.

7. When you have finished, let your leaf bowl dry well.

8. When the leaves are all dry, turn the leaf bowl right side up and gently pull the plastic bowl out. Your leaf bowl is now ready for its soil and seeds. When you have added your soil and seeds, place your Scented Leaf Basket indoors in a sunny spot, such as a windowsill, so that the seeds will have the light they need to grow.

   Remember to always water your soil very lightly so that your leaf bowl does not become too soggy.

Personalized Nature Portrait

Ages 6 and under

Have you ever visited a museum of art or an art gallery? Maybe your school has a wall where the projects from your art classes are displayed. You've probably discovered that art includes many different textures and shapes as well as colors. The earth is a giant work of art with many colors, textures, shapes, and sizes. A personalized nature portrait combines your own artistic style with the earth's materials to create a portrait of who you are with what nature made.

Adult supervision required

Materials

Bag for collecting nature materials
1 8½ × 11–inch piece cardboard
String, twine, or shoelace, 24 inches long
Pencil
Rubber cement

1. Begin with a walk outdoors. Take along your bag for collecting. Gather from the ground small pieces of bark, small stones, twigs, leaves, dried grasses, or anything you can find that is small enough to fit in the palm of your hand.

2. When you return from your nature walk, use your pencil and draw a picture of yourself on the piece of cardboard. This can be a picture of you from your shoulders up or a picture of your entire body.

3. Ask an adult to help you punch two small holes in the two upper corners of the cardboard. Poke the end of the twine through one of the holes and then through the other.

4. Tie the ends of the twine tightly together, creating a loop for hanging your portrait.

5. Using the materials from your collecting bag, fill in your portrait. If you like, also fill in the background. You may decide to use leaves for your hair and grasses for your skin or small pieces of bark for your eyes and nose. You can even choose to put smaller items on top of bigger ones to add color and shape. Move around and experiment with the different pieces you have collected until you are happy with the final portrait.

6. When you are finished, use the rubber cement to carefully glue down all of the nature pieces on your portrait. Be sure you use enough rubber cement to hold firm the heavier pieces such as the bark or twigs.

7. Let your portrait dry for a day. Then, use the twine loop to hang your Personalized Nature Portrait on a wall for everyone to admire.

Leaf Literature Art

Ages 7 and up

Many great artists, such as Thomas Cole (1801–1848), Claude Monet (1840–1926), and Vincent van Gogh (1853–1890), and writers, such as President Thomas Jefferson (1743–1846) and Henry David Thoreau (1817–1862), have been inspired by the earth's natural beauty. You don't have to be famous to turn your feelings about nature into art. Get a pencil and paper, and take a walk outdoors. Look at all the natural things around you. How does it make you feel? Imagine how different it would be without any green grass to lie in, scented flowers to smell, or tall trees for shade? How would that make you feel? Now sit quietly and think about the beautiful things you have seen along your walk. Take a moment to write down your thoughts. You can write your thoughts out in sentences, a story, or a poem. Or you can write about what you have seen

and heard. Along your journey be sure to collect several leaves, about a dozen of all shapes, sizes, and colors, to include in your Leaf Literature Art. Now you are ready to turn your thoughts into beautiful leaf literature art that will express your love for nature and encourage others to appreciate nature, too!

Materials

2 sheets newspaper
2 8½ × 11–inch sheets white watercolor paper, sketchpad paper, or thick construction paper
Paintbrush, 1 inch or wider
Set of watercolor paints in assorted colors, or you can use regular paints with a lot of water
1 cup water
Fine-point black marker or pen
Craft glue or homemade Natural Glue, p. xiv
12 leaves
Plastic container
Picture frame with 8½ × 11–inch opening

1. Take the sheets of newspaper. Spread them flat on a table or workspace.
2. Lay one sheet of watercolor paper or thick construction paper on top of the newspaper. Color

the paper with the paintbrush. Paint the paper with any design and as many colors you like. Be sure to cover the entire sheet of paper with many colors and let it dry completely.

3. Clean off your paintbrush and let it dry.

4. When the paper is completely dry, turn the paper upright so that the shorter sides are at the top and bottom.

5. Using the black marker or pen, very neatly copy the sentences, poem, or story you wrote during your nature walk. Write sentences across the paper, from left to right, leaving at least 2 inches between each line. You may want to write out your thoughts in pencil first. This will help you to know how much room you'll need. You don't have to write your words perfectly straight. This is a work of art, and art means that it is created by you, so it can be any way you like. Let the marker dry completely so that it will not smudge when you handle it in the next step.

6. When dry, slowly tear the lines of copy into strips of paper. Do this slowly and carefully so that you don't tear through your words. The edges of each strip of paper should not be perfectly straight, but jagged and rough.

7. Lay your clean piece of watercolor paper on your newspaper. Using a few drops of craft glue on the back of these strips, attach the colored strips of paper onto the clean piece of watercolor paper. Be sure to glue them in the order in which it has been written so that it can be read just the way you wrote it. You can glue the colored strips straight across or at an angle, whichever you prefer.

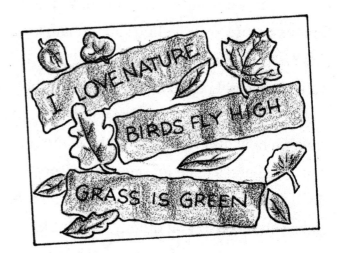

8. Now place the leaves you collected onto the paper any way you like. Be sure not to cover any of your writing. You don't have to use all of the leaves.

9. In the plastic container mix about 1 tablespoon of the craft glue with 1 tablespoon of water to thin out the glue.

10. Dip your paintbrush into the glue and water mixture and then paint over the top of your leaves. Make sure to coat some of the paper around the leaves so that everything will stick.

11. Let your Leaf Literature Art dry completely.

12. When it is dry, place it in your picture frame so that you can hang up your Leaf Literature Art on the wall. You can also make smaller Leaf Literature Art, $3\frac{1}{2} \times 5$ inches or 5×7 inches. These can be placed in smaller picture frames that will fit on a desk, shelf, or, mantel or can be given to others as a nature gift.

🌐 Earth Action

Tree Helpers

You can help save the forests! You don't have to be a great scientist to make a difference. If you take a small step, you can help make a big difference. Just think how much good we could do if everyone in the world took one small step every day. We could save millions of trees! Here are some small steps you can take:

🌿 Reuse grocery bags or take a cloth bag when you go shopping at the store. Sometimes stores will give you money back for bringing your own shopping bags.

🌿 Wrap gifts with old newspaper and decorate them with a bright fabric ribbon. Once the present has been opened, you can reuse the newspaper for craft projects.

🌿 Use cloth napkins and towels instead of paper ones.

🌿 Print, paint, and color on the back of paper you have already used.

Some great places to write for more ideas on how to save the forests include: Rainforest Action Network, is 221 Pine Street, 5th Floor, San Francisco, CA 94104 (www.ran.org) and the Sierra Club, 85 Second Street, 2nd Floor, San Francisco, CA 94105 (www.sierra club.org).

2

Rocks, Pebbles, and Shells

Rocks, pebbles, and shells all play an important part in making the earth a home. Rocks are formed by three different factors—stress, pressure, and heat. *Stress* is when one thing pushes or pulls another. *Pressure* is when something is pressed by something else. *Heat* is the extra energy a thing gains when it gets hotter, making it get bigger. Some rocks, such as *sedimentary* (said-i-MEN-tary) rocks, are formed when various sediments that sink to the bottom of water, such as sand, shell, or mud, are put under great stress, or force, and eventually fuse together into a rock. Heat forms rocks that are called *igneous* (IG-ne-ous). These rocks are made when hot magma (melted rock) from the center of the earth, or lava from a volcano, cools. And *metamorphic* (meh-ta-MORE-fic) rocks are formed out of sedimentary and igneous rocks after they have been put under more pressure and heat. The ground we walk on is made up of layers and layers of these different types of rock. Some rocks are very large, such as cliffs, volcanoes, and mountains. These giant rocks provide caves for bears to hibernate in (sleeping away the cold months of the year), and mountains for eagles to build their nests and mountain lions to roam. Just as trees grow tall, lose branches and leaves, and change colors over their life span, rocks change, too. Mostly, rocks change on the outside when events in their natural environment cause them to change. Rain, snow, and wind are just some of the environmental forces that change rocks. It takes a lot of wind, water, and wear to break down great big mountains into small rocks and tiny pebbles. This process of breaking down giant rock into smaller pieces is called *erosion* (ee-ROW-shun). Many years of wind and rain beating down on a cliff can produce tiny smooth rocks called pebbles that are found at the bottom of the cliff or wash up on a seashore. Imagine, a little pebble the size of your fingernail could have once been bigger than you! The rocks and pebbles you'll use here in *Organic Crafts* are small enough for you to hold in your hand.

Rock Your World

Ages 7 and up

Our earth is made up of a lot of rock and water covering the rocky ocean floor. The ground we walk on is rock that has pushed its way up out of the water, creating land. There is rock underneath everything on earth, whether mountains covered with grass, forest floors covered with moss and soil, or desert dunes filled with sand. Because of all the rock that has moved over time, our world is not a smooth, flat surface. Instead it is spherical, peppered with giant mountains, cliffs, valleys, and fields. A great way to see the surface of the earth is to look at a relief globe. A *relief globe* is a globe with a three-dimensional (3-D) raised surface. You can run your fingers along the surface. The mountains feel like little bumps. The ocean shoreline has a wavy surface. This gives the globe a bumpy feel, or texture, which is another dimension added to a flat surface. In this activity you'll make your own relief globe, and it's going to Rock Your World.

Materials

2 large paperclips
1 Styrofoam ball or 1 sheet newspaper crunched up
    into a ball at least 4–5 inches in diameter
2 sheets blue construction paper

Rubber cement

Small plastic butter tub or other plastic container
  smaller than your Styrofoam or newspaper ball

Map of the world*

10 small, flat rocks of various shapes and sizes

*See the *National Geographic Picture Atlas of Our World.* Washington, DC: National Geographic Society, 1990. It has a map that's just the right size for this project on pages 11 and 12. This book is also a great resource for all projects connected to the globe, and it offers help in understanding maps.

1. Push one large paperclip through the top of your Styrofoam or newspaper ball. Do the same with the other paperclip on the opposite end (bottom) of the ball. These paperclips represent the earth's axis on which your globe can spin. The *axis* is an imaginary line that runs from the South Pole through the center of the earth to the North Pole. The earth's axis is tilted so that the sun does not shine on the planet the same way every day of the year. As the earth spins round and round on its tilted axis each day and revolves around the sun each year, we experience the different types of weather of the seasons.

2. Crunch up your blue construction paper into a ball. Spread it flat.

3. Cover one side of the construction paper with rubber cement. Cover the Styrofoam or newspaper ball with the wrinkled-up construction paper. Be sure to cover the foam or newspaper ball entirely. The paper should remain wrinkled, because this is your wavy ocean floor.

4. Next, place your blue ocean ball on the plastic tub to dry. The tub will hold the ball in place while you glue down your continents. Using your map of the world as a guide, glue each rock to the blue ball where you think a continent should be. Attach with the rubber cement. Remember: a work of art is never exact, so do your best to make it your own design.

5. Let the rocks dry completely. Then, hold on to both paperclips and gently spin your world around, just as our earth spins on its axis. Rock Your World!

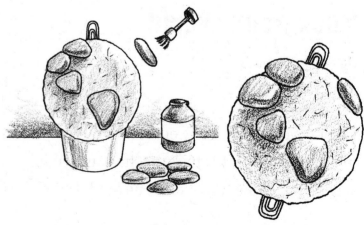

Rock Sculpture

Ages 6 and under

As we have learned, art is not just a picture painted on paper. Art can be two-dimensional, or even three-dimensional like a giant sculpture or clay vase. One of the earth's most magnificent rock sculptures lies underground in caves. These caves contain many different rock formations called stalactites, stalagmites, soda straws, and cave pearls. These strange and beautiful formations are the results of water working through rock to create nature's own sculptures. When rainwater flows underground, it mixes with other natural chemicals to work away at the rocks. It gradually smoothes them and makes new shapes. After time, underground caves and rock formations are left behind.

To learn more about natural rock sculptures and caves, check out *Caves* by Rachel Lynette. Detroit, MI: KidHaven Press, 2005.

Of course one rock alone, with its different sides and angles, is its own rock

Nature Notes

Stonehenge

Thousands of years ago people in England built a giant circle of rocks we call Stonehenge. No one is exactly sure who built this ring of stone or how such big stones could have been moved and placed on top of one another. Some of the stones weigh about 30 tons, which is about as heavy as a dozen or more elephants! That's an amazing amount of weight to move before the creation of machinery to help move such large objects. When looking at the circle of giant rocks, you will see three different types of rocks coming together to form sculptures. The smaller rocks, called bluestones, contain green, blue, and gray colors. There are 82 bluestone rocks standing about 8 feet high within the circle. There are also very tall rock blocks about 18 feet high, called *sarsens*, that are made from sandstone, one of the hardest rocks of all. The third type of rock structure found in the formation is smaller sarsens, called *lintels*. There are many legends and stories about why and how Stonehenge was constructed. Some people once believed that the rocks had magically appeared from the earth; others believe that hundreds of people built it as a place of worship. One thing most everyone agrees is that Stonehenge is a beautiful and amazing sculpture made out of stone. To learn more about Stonehenge, check out www.stonehenge.co.uk.

sculpture. When we put several rocks together, there will be even more sizes, colors, textures, and shapes to admire. A Rock Sculpture is a way to display all the interesting characteristics of rocks.

Materials

1 small, flat piece wood or large flat rock for base of sculpture

Mosaic tile adhesive (available at craft supply stores)

10 small rocks and pebbles, different colors, shapes, sizes

1. Start with the wood base and add a little mosaic tile adhesive where you want to place your first rock. It might be easier to use the bigger rocks at the bottom, because they are so heavy.
2. Place a rock on top of the glue and hold it firmly in place for at least 2 minutes. Let the rock dry for another minute or two before adding more.
3. Add glue to the top of the first rock or next to the first rock and place another rock there. You may want to let a few of the rocks dry firmly before building your rock sculpture higher. You can build an animal, a mountain, a castle, or even your own vision of Stonehenge.

4. When it is completely done, let your Rock Sculpture dry overnight.

Rock Racers

Ages 7 and up

We now know that rocks can change, but did you know they can also move? This is known as the rock cycle. Rocks, and all the tiny parts of rocks, move and shift over time. Some of this movement comes from environmental influences, such as wind, rain, or animals.

Rocks may move when a bear rolls one out of its path, or when the rain washes one out into a body of water, or when the winds blow tiny pebbles across the desert. Rocks also move as the earth's crust moves. The earth's crust is made up of giant rock slabs called tectonic plates that fit together like a great big jigsaw puzzle. But these plates will move around and change as magma from the earth's core rises up and overflows out of a volcano. When there's an earthquake, the plates may pull apart and make deep cracks in the earth's surface called *rifts*. The plates may even bump together, overlap, or push upward making new mountains. With all this movement of the earth's crust, more rock is pushed and moved and rolled around. Some rocks will disappear back under the earth's crust. Others may just roll away to a new home. Much like the work of art our earth makes as it moves and changes and rolls rocks all around, Rock Racers is a way to move rocks around.

Rock Racers is not only fun to play, but is a work of art, too. When you see your finished game, you will want to set it up where everyone can see the cool designs you have created.

Materials

Bucket
50 or more small, flat rocks
Water
Old towel
1 piece foam board, at least 8½ × 11 inches
Pencil
Rubber cement
2 or more bottle caps

1. Start by collecting 50 or more small, flat rocks in your bucket.
2. Wash your rocks and lay them on an old towel to dry. A pebble, rock, or shell with a clean surface will stick better.
3. Set down your foam board and draw at least two wavy lines from top to bottom. Each wavy line should be different from the other. These will be the racing tracks for your bottle caps.
4. Outline the racing tracks with rocks, making sure that the space between the rock outlines is at least 2 inches wide so that your bottle cap fits through.

Mining Minerals

Minerals and gems are types of rocks and pebbles. The difference between a mineral and a rock is that a *mineral* contains only *one* material, or substance, such as quartz, whereas a rock has many different substances combined. A *gem* is a type of mineral that sparkles and has a pretty color. Once this mineral is cut and polished it becomes a beautiful gem, such as a diamond or emerald. Gems are valuable because of their beauty and also because they are rare. You can search for gems, minerals, and pretty rocks in a river, stream, pond, marsh, or swamp. You will find them by separating them out from the water with a pan. Ask an adult to use a screwdriver or nail to poke several holes through an old tin or aluminum pie pan. When you put your pan under the moving water you will find many things, such as rocks, pebbles, sand, and water creatures, like water spiders, tadpoles, and minnows. If you're lucky, you might also find gold. Remember to always ask an adult to go with you when you are near water.

To learn more about rocks and minerals, check out *Geology Rocks! 50 Hands-on Activities to Explore the Earth* by Cindy Blobaum. Charlotte, VT: Williamson, 1999.

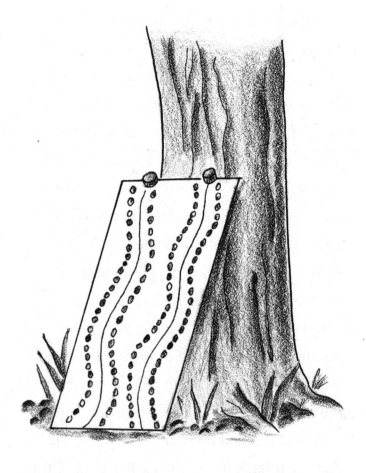

5. With the rubber cement, glue down your rocks. Use plenty of rubber cement so they will stay in place when the game board is moved.
6. Let the rocks dry overnight.
7. When the rocks have dried, tilt your board upside down and sideways to see if there are

any loose rocks. If a rock falls off, reglue it and let it dry before continuing.

8. When the board is completely dry, you are ready to race a friend from top to bottom. Lean the board at an angle against a tree or wall. Each player should hold a bottle cap at the top of the board inside the rock tracks. When someone says go, let go of your bottle caps and watch them race to the finish. When you are not using your Rock Racers board, set it up where people can see the design you've made.

Rock 'n' Desk Set

Ages 7 and up

Every rock that you find on your nature walks may hold a special memory for you. A smooth rock may be one you saved from skimming the pond with a friend. A blue-colored rock may be one from a visit to the shore. All of your rock treasures, both rocks and gems (real or pretend), can be used to decorate almost everything, including the place where you do your homework—your desk. Fill your desk with memories and art by making a collection of Rock 'n' Desk Set.

Materials

1 cardboard box, about 3 × 3 inches
Scissors
Aluminum can
1 piece construction paper
Craft glue or homemade Natural Glue, p. xiv
Collection of rocks, gems, and pebbles
Mosaic tile adhesive

1. First, build your desk set. Cut out two sides of your cardboard box. This will be your letter and paper holder.
2. Cover your aluminum can with the piece of construction paper, cutting and gluing it to fit. This will be your pencil cup.
3. Put several drops of mosaic tile adhesive on the holder. Press the rocks, gems, and pebbles in place.
4. Do this until the entire holder and pencil cup are covered.
5. Let dry. Then decorate your desk with this Rock 'n' Desk Set.

Pebble Pendant

Ages 7 and up

Most jewels come from the earth. Whether it's turquoise from Arizona or gold from Mexico, rocks, gems, shells, and minerals are all part of nature's jewelry box. The jewelry you see in stores has been broken down or polished into smooth stones, much as wind and rain break and polish rocks into smaller pebbles. This process is called *weathering*. You can make your own nature jewelry out of the pretty and colorful pebbles you find on the ground. You can polish the pebbles you select the natural way: rub the pebble against another rock, roll it in sand, use a tumbler to rinse it in, or wash it with water to smooth the surface and make it shine. You can also paint it with clear fingernail polish to make it shiny.

Pebble Pendant will help you to turn your pretty pebble into a pendant that hangs from a necklace.

Materials

¼ cup clay dug up outdoors* or air-dry modeling clay

1 metal key ring

Collection of small pretty pebbles

1. Add a little water to the clay. Work it between your hands until it forms a soft ball.
2. Form the clay ball into the shape of a large peanut about 2 inches tall.
3. Press the metal key ring into the top part of your clay peanut. Gently mold the clay around it, leaving the center hole open. This will be the ring that you can thread a chain or string through to wear.
4. Put a pebble in the center of the bottom portion of your clay peanut. Be sure to press it firmly into the clay so that it will be held tightly. You can add more pebbles if you want to fill the clay pendant.

*Different types of clay are found in different regional locations. Often, red clay can be found about 12 inches below grass and dirt. When digging becomes difficult, clay is usually the reason. In addition, dark gray clay can be found near swamps or where coal is found. If you use clay from the ground, have an adult help you to locate it and dig it up. Your clay from the ground doesn't have to be clay alone. In fact, soil and mud mixed into the clay can help prevent your pendant from cracking.

5. Place your pendant in the sun to dry for at least 8 hours or until the pebble is stuck firmly to the clay.

6. When it is completely dry, you can slide it onto a string or chain and wear it as jewelry, making it a Pebble Pendant.

Pebble Party Shakers

Ages 6 and under

Pebbles seem to be everywhere—in driveways, along beaches, on the playground at school. Do you think taking one handful of pebbles from our earth makes a big difference? What if all of us helped ourselves to a handful of pebbles, a barrel of sand, or an entire tree? Sometimes our earth's landscape is damaged as we dig for more materials and resources. Rock, stone, and pebble quarries (mines) are human-made places where natural resources seem plentiful. But a quarry is one example of a way we change our landscape by removing trees and dirt, and digging through rock for more construction resources. What about reusing materials we already have, such as stone and bricks from a building no longer in use? Although we may also borrow many materials from the earth for our nature crafts, we should clean them and return as many as possible to their original locations when we are finished.

This craft is a simple example of how you can borrow nature's materials and return them to the earth when you're done. Pebble Party Shakers are easy to make and can be used as noisemakers for any celebration including birthdays, the Fourth of July, and New Year's Eve.

Materials

1 sheet construction paper, any color, any size
Scissors
Colorful stickers, crayons, or colored markers
Craft glue or homemade Natural Glue, p. xiv
2 empty pop cans
Handful of pebbles
2 sheets aluminum foil, each 5 × 5 inches
4 rubber bands
12 or more pieces raffia, twine, or ribbon, each at least 12 inches long

1. Cut the construction paper lengthwise.
2. Decorate the construction paper with stickers, markers, and crayons.
3. Put glue on the back of a construction paper strip and wrap it around one pop can. Repeat for second can.

4. Let the paper dry.
5. Fill both pop cans with the pebbles. Cover the open end of each pop can with an aluminum foil sheet.
6. Place two rubber bands around a foil to secure the cover in place.
7. Wrap a few strands of raffia or ribbons around the top and bottom of each can and tie in place. Your Pebble Party Shakers are now ready to shake, shake, shake!

Be sure to recycle the cans, foil, and pebbles when you've finished shaking.

Pebble Puppets

Ages 6 and under

Create an earth art puppet show with materials you find outside. From scary lions to wacky-looking people, you can add to your puppet collection after each nature walk you take. With just a few pebbles you can create Pebble Puppets to look like anything you wish.

Materials

1 sheet cardboard, any size or color (try an empty cereal box)

Scissors

Craft glue or homemade Natural Glue, p. xiv

1 wooden craft stick for each puppet you want to make

Rubber cement

5 or more pebbles for each puppet

Collection of materials from nature, such as tall grasses, leaves, dandelions, and flower petals

1. Begin by making the pattern for your puppets. Cut out a circle from the cardboard. Try tracing around the bottom of a can or cap with a pencil to get a nice shape.
2. Use the glue to attach the cardboard circle to the top portion of a wooden craft stick. Add some pebbles for eyes and maybe a mouth using the rubber cement.
3. While your pebbles are drying, think about all the puppets you could make. You could put gold and brown leaves all around the circle and make a lion. Or you could glue some pieces of grass along the top of the circle and create a person with spiky hair.

4. Take your ideas and put them to work by gluing the collection of nature materials on to your Pebble Puppets. Use your imagination. When you walk in the wilderness, think of all the things you could create with materials from the earth.

Pebble Pot

Ages 6 and under

Can you press down on a pebble and change its shape? How about if you cooked it like they do in the book *Stone Soup: An Old Tale* by Marcia Brown. New York: Aladdin, 2005? You probably won't have much luck, but the earth certainly can. In fact, it changes the shape of pebbles by pressing *and* cooking them every day. Remember that one of the three types of rocks we call metamorphic is shaped when the earth puts more heat and pressure on a rock. This eventually changes its shape and structure.

A Pebble Pot is an easy way to display hair accessories, small toys, or spare change, and it is a great idea to help keep things in one place and looking great. A pebble pot is a great place for a potted plant for flowers. It is a wonderful gift for anyone, especially when made by you.

Materials

Bucket
50 or more colored and unusual-shaped pebbles
1 sheet old newspaper
1 old plastic tub or clay pot
1 large stone or book
Rubber cement
A handful of sand

1. Take the bucket and go on a pebble hunt. In your bucket, collect each pebble or group of pebbles that catches your eye. Fill your bucket so that you will have many pebbles to choose from.
2. Spread the sheet of newspaper on a table or workspace.
3. Set your tub or pot on the newspaper. Put the book or stone under one side of the tub so that it tilts back.
4. Cover the section of the tub or pot that is tilted upward with rubber cement. Put pebbles all over this section. Spinkle with sand
5. Let dry.
6. Move your tub slightly so another section is tilted up.
7. Cover that section with rubber cement, pebbles, and a sprinkling of sand. Let dry.
8. Continue this until the entire tub or pot is covered with pebbles and sand.
9. Let all the glued pebbles and sand dry completely. Then put your Pebble Pot to use!

She (or He) Paints Seashells

Ages 6 and under

Seashells have great colors, from browns to reds and even purples and pinks. These colors often are the result of the type of food eaten by the mollusk living inside the shell. Some of the mollusks that live inside seashells produce more colors than found in their shells. The murex snail of the tropics, with its spiky, hornlike shell, produces a substance that can turn cloth a beautiful purple color. Long ago, before the creation of human-made paint, this colored dye was once very valuable and therefore was only used by kings and queens. There is a story that the purple color of a murex snail was discovered by Queen Helen of Troy's dog. Chewing on it dyed his mouth purple! Although we should no longer use snails or any living creatures to make color dye, we can play with our own colorful nature paints and crayons to bring the sea to the shore with painted seashell art!

You can learn more about the exciting world of seashells at www.earthsky.org/article/seashells or www.seashells.org.

Materials

1 small piece foam board, 5 × 5 inches, any color
Scissors
Large screwdriver
1 piece twine, 12 inches
Enough seashells to cover the foam board
Watercolor paints, or box of crayons in browns, reds, oranges, greens, and blues (can substitute Nature's Paints, see page 70, or cornstarch paint, p. xv)
Mosaic tile adhesive or rubber cement

1. Using the scissors, poke two holes into the top of your foam board, 1 inch in from each side.
2. Poke the screwdriver through the same holes, making them large enough to pull the twine through. Ask an adult for help with this step.
3. Push each end of the twine through the holes and tie together. Now your foam board will hang when you are finished.

🐾 Nature Notes

Super Shells

Shells come in a variety of sizes, colors, and shapes. They are pretty to look at and fun to collect, but they also have super powers! Shells are the homes of soft-bodied creatures that live in water or moist places—for example, turtles, crabs, and mollusks, such as snails and clams. Shells have the power to protect animals by hiding them from *predators* (other creatures that may eat them), such as frogs, snakes, and birds. Since shells are so pretty to look at and have many different shapes and colors, they are also used by people as decorations in wall art, sewn into clothing, and turned into jewelry. In some cultures they are exchanged as a form of money.

"Cling Ons"

Sometimes it's safer and easier for an animal to stay in one place and hide while waiting for food. Some animals, such as oysters, barnacles, limpets, and mussels, do just that. These creatures live inside seashells. They protect themselves from being bashed against the shore by a wave or being eaten by other creatures by attaching themselves to rocks, larger shells, boats, and buoys that are floated in waterways. Some of these creatures produce a sticky substance that helps them cling to a hard surface. Others, such as the limpet, have a strong muscular foot that holds it firmly in place. When waves rush by, these shelled creatures cling on, hide from predators, and wait for food to be brought to them.

4. Paint one side of your seashells using watercolors or crayons. Decorate the shells any way you like. You can draw pictures on them or stripes, dots, or patterns and even write your name. When you are done painting your seashells, you are ready to glue them on to your board.

5. Using the mosaic tile adhesive or rubber cement, carefully apply glue to the unpainted sides of your shells. Press each shell firmly in place on the board. Do this for all of your shells until the board is covered.

6. When the adhesive dries, you can hang up your painted seashell art. Or give it to someone as a gift, so that they'll know of you that She (or He) Paints Seashells!

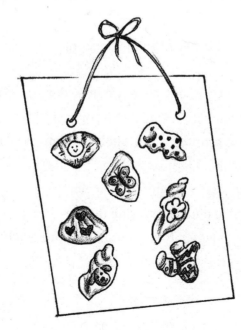

Muscle Man

Ages 7 and up

A mussel is a fresh water and ocean animal that lives in a shell. It has two blackish, long, thin shells that open and close like a clam's. Mussels are a type of cling-on shelled creature that produces sticky threads called *byssi*. These sticky threads help mussels hold on tightly to rocks. Because they can hold on so strongly, maybe they should have been called muscles, just like the ones on the Muscle Man created in this craft.

Materials

4 mussels, 8 shells all together (Remember that they have two wing-like shells.)

1 brick air-dry modeling clay or 1 cup clay dug up from the earth*

Ruler

2 tiny pebbles for the eyes

2 flat rocks

*If you use clay from the ground, have an adult help you to locate and dig it up. Your clay from the ground does not have to be perfect; the soil and mud mixed with clay can help prevent cracking when it dries.

1. Form five balls from your modeling clay, each about 1 inch around in size.

2. Slowly roll out four of the balls until they look like 4-inch pencils. Use the ruler to check the length of each.

3. Gently clamp one mussel over each tube of clay. Be sure not to break the clay, but leave a little clay sticking out on each end.

4. Lay out each piece in the shape of a person, with two muscled arms and two muscled legs.

5. Pinch the clay ends together in the middle to form a body.

6. Add the last ball to the top for the head.

7. Place two tiny pebbles on the head for eyes.

8. When your Muscle Man is ready, stand him up on the two flat rocks.

9. Push the clay on the rocks so that he can have feet. Now your Muscle Man is ready to sit in a sunny spot to dry and become even stronger!

Garden Chimes

Ages 7 and up

Shells make different noises when they are clapped together. When they dangle from a string they make musical sounds. Garden chimes make pretty music when the wind blows through them. They also keep unwanted pests away from the vegetables and flowers in your garden.

Adult supervision required

Materials

Power drill, for use by an adult only
Pair of work gloves or heavy-duty gardening gloves
Safety goggles
12 seashells
Scissors
Spool of twine or string
2 twigs, 12 inches or longer

1. Ask an adult to drill a small hole in each of the seashells. The adult should wear the work gloves to protect his or her hands as he or she hold the shell steady. Be sure that everyone around the

drill wears safety goggles. By using a very small drill bit the shells will not break. You can drill a hole anywhere on the shell. If you drill closer to an edge, the shell will dangle better.

2. Cut four pieces of twine or string, each at least 12 inches long.

3. Poke one of the strings through the hole in the seashell. Thread it on the string.

4. Tie a knot under the seashell to hold it in place. Thread another seashell on the same sting. Tie a knot under the seashell to hold it in place. Do this once more with the same string. You will have three shells tied to your string. When you hold the string up with the last knot on the bottom, your seashells will stay in place. Follow the same method for the three other pieces of twine or string, using three seashells on each string.

5. Cut several feet of twine or string. Tie the two twigs together. Do this by laying the string flat across a table, then setting one twig up and down, crossing the string in the center. The next twig should be laid on top of the first to form a cross.

6. Tie the string loosely over the two twigs at their meeting point.

7. Wrap each end of the string around the opposite corner in its diagonal direction.

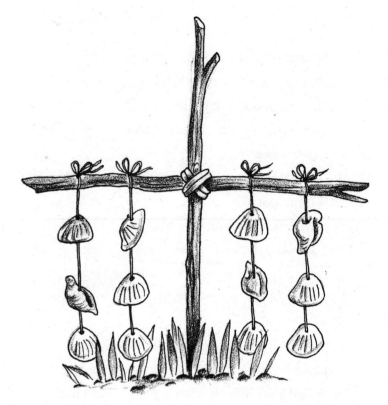

8. When you come to the end of your string, tuck the ends under the wrapped string or simply tie another knot. The twigs should form a sturdy cross shape.

9. On each arm of your crossed twigs, tie two of your shell strings so that the shell knots are at the bottom. Place these strings close enough together to hit one another when the wind blows. When you are done, stand your Garden Chimes outdoors and listen for the wind to make its magic music.

Shadow Box Collection

Ages 7 and up

A shadow box is used to display important things, such as pictures, a collection of items, or an award. A rock, shell, or pebble collection is something that can be displayed as art with the use of just a few household objects to make a creative Shadow Box Collection.

Adult supervision required

Materials

Collection of small boxes, such as cut-open juice
    boxes* or jewelry boxes, including tops and
    bottoms
Scissors
Assorted crayons and markers
Acrylic or Nature's Paints, page 70, or Cornstarch
    Paints, page xv)
Small paintbrush
1 cup water
Rag

*Ask an adult to help you cut open empty juice boxes. Gently place the tip of the scissors into the front center of the box and cut away the front panel.

Craft glue or homemade Natural Glue, p. xiv
Clothespins
Collection of rocks, shells, or pebbles
Rubber cemen

1. Decorate your boxes, inside or outside, anyway you like with the markers, crayons, and paints. One suggestion would be to paint the outside edges of the boxes and color the inside with the markers, creating designs or patterns. You may also want to write inside the boxes the names of places where you found your collection of pebbles, shells, and rocks. For example, "Laguna Beach," "my backyard in Chicago," "Sue's House," "on a walk with my dog," and so forth. Doing this will make your shadow box extra-special, because the labels will remind you of times you've shared with people and fun places you've visited.

2. Once the boxes are decorated and dry, arrange them to form a giant box shape. They should all be flat on the table with the openings facing up so that you can place your collection inside. The arrangement of the boxes when laid side by side does not have to be in a box pattern. In fact, the more unusual the pattern, the more artistic the shadow boxes will be.

🌐 *Earth Action*

Rock Rescue

Many people throughout the world are teaming together to protect rocks and the history they hold. People who study rocks are called *geologists*. *Historical geologists* look at how the earth changes and how events on earth have changed the way rocks look. Different shapes of rocks, such as the naturally formed Grand Canyon, or those built by people long ago, such as Stonehenge or the Great Pyramids of Egypt, teach us many things about our history and the history of the earth. Rocks with *fossils* (lasting impressions left in the earth of once-living things) teach us about the kind of animal and plant life that lived long ago. They teach us, for instance, about the tyrannosaurus dinosaur, or about plants like the cycad, and about animals like the woolly rhino, all of which no longer exist. When plants or animal bones are buried along with rocks under the weight of dirt or sand, an impression forms, giving us a peek at the life that once existed in that spot. Rocks also tell us a lot about what types of nonliving things, such as minerals and natural resources, are nearby. For example, when you see dark bands or seams running through rock walls, coal-bearing rocks typically have formed. Coal is a natural resource used for fuel. We need rocks to educate us about our earth's past and to help us to predict the future.

3. When you are happy with your design, glue the sides of the boxes together with the glue. Hold them together with the clothes pins. Let dry completely.

4. Use the rubber cement to affix each rock, shell, or pebble inside the boxes.

5. When everything is completely dry, you can hang this on a wall or set it on a bookshelf for everyone to admire. Your Shadow Box Collection will be a work of art and a display of your adventures all in one place.

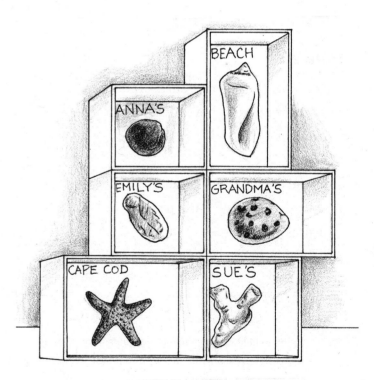

3
Soil, Clay, and Sand

If you go outside and scoop up a handful of dirt, you will be holding hundreds of living organisms. An *organism* is something that is alive. It can be smaller than an ant or larger than a tree. The dirt beneath your feet is constantly moving. It is filled with millions of tiny living things. These include plantlike organisms that live in the water called *algae*, tiny spider like animals known as mites, the hardworking one-celled organisms called *bacteria*, earthworms, and, of course, all the mushrooms, molds, and other types of fungi that break down dead plants and animals. All of these tiny organisms live off one another right below our feet. As they move around in the dirt, they mix air with water and with tiny pieces of dead plants and animals. All the organisms moving around mix up the dirt and turn it into rich, fertile soil that nourishes other plants and animals to help them live. Wind, building construction, and daily wear from people and animals erode the topsoil, making it difficult for new plants to grow and animals to feed. (Remember that *erosion*, as we learned in chapter 2, means the wearing away of something or making it smaller by gradually tearing it apart.) One way to protect precious topsoil against erosion is by planting trees and composting. The roots of strong trees hold soil firmly in place and guard against wind erosion. Composting is a way to make more soil and dirt. *Composting* involves mixing natural materials, such as food scraps and grass clippings, which break down over time when mixed with air. These materials eventually become rich new dirt that can help to nourish a garden or lawn, or simply reduce waste.

Homemade Soil

Ages 7 and up

Composting makes soil rich with nutrients, and rich soil helps plants grow. Instead of just throwing things away, you can reduce the amount of waste you produce by recycling (see chapter 6, "Reduce, Reuse, and Recycle") and by composting your food scraps to help the environment. In this activity you'll learn how to create your own Homemade Soil.

Adult supervision required

Materials

Gardening gloves
Shovel
Chicken wire, 8 feet long
Gallon size watering can, filled with water

1. Ask your parents for permission to use a space in your backyard for a compost pile. Select a place away from your home's entrance or windows, because the decaying food and grass is smelly. If you live in an apartment, ask the property manager whether you can have a space for composting. Explain that you will be making new fertile soil, which can be used in gardens or window boxes. Your neighbors may help by giving you their yard waste. If you can't compost at home, you may want to ask your teacher at school. Most schools welcome composting as a class project.

2. Always put on gardening gloves to protect your hands before working with wire or gardening tools.

3. Begin by clearing the area you will be composting in. Pull weeds, and smooth out the dirt or rocks below.

4. Check with your town to see if any wires or cables are underground before you dig. This step is very important to prevent you and others from being hurt.

5. If you want to make your Homemade Soil below ground, have an adult help you dig a hole that is at least 3 × 3 × 3 feet. If you would like to make Homemade Soil above ground, there is no need to dig a hole. Instead, place the chicken wire in a

ring and press it firmly into the ground. You'll need thick protective gloves to use chicken wire. It's thin wire and very flexible (will bend easily). Gently push the ends into the ground, or dig down a couple of inches, hold the wire in place, and then pack dirt around the bottom to secure the fencing. You can expand the wire as you add more items to your compost pile. Simply push it back into place when you remove some of your new healthy soil.

6. Now for the fun part: every day you can gather food and table scraps from your meals and put them in your compost hole or ring. Great things to add are leftover vegetables and fruit, coffee grounds, and eggshells. Never add meat, bones, or bread products, because they will attract unwanted animals and pests.

7. Add grass clippings from mowing and weeds pulled from your lawn or neighborhood, or any yard waste. Anything that is from nature can be added to your compost pile. Be sure not to add big clumps of grass without mixing in twigs and leaves, because grass can rot, become slimy, and attract flies. If you find an earthworm wiggling around looking for a home, gently put it in your compost pile. Earthworms are a big help when composting because they help to make soil. With their wiggly bodies they dig tunnels through soil, loosening it up and allowing air to flow through. You and your earthworm will be very happy with the result!

8. Each week add about half a watering can of water to your compost and mix with a shovel. If your compost pile becomes too wet or it has been raining a lot, stop adding water. Instead add more dry ingredients, such as leaves and twigs. Your compost pile should never be soggy; it should look crumbly like soil.

In a few months your compost will have turned into Homemade Soil that you can use to grow new plants.

Dirty Facts

Almost 100 percent of our food comes from the soil that makes up the earth's crust—the top layer of soil found under the surface or just underground. The type of soil, whether thick and hard like clay, coarse like sand, or soft like topsoil, plays a big part in determining the types of plants that will grow. Clay allows very little water to pass through it, so plants must have strong roots and require very little air movement to grow in clay. Plants growing in clay also need a lot of water. Because the particles in clay-filled soil are packed so tightly, it holds water well. Clay is often found by riverbanks and shallow lakes. Geraniums and hollyhocks can grow well in clay. Willow trees also love all the water that is held by clay-rich soil. Sand allows water to pass right through, so plants requiring very little water do well in sandy soil. Alyssum is a plant that can grow well in sandy soil. Of course, cacti, which love dry conditions, are often found in sandy areas. Thick topsoil that is a rich brown color and soft to the touch holds water well. It has many nutrients to feed all kinds of plants, such as sturdy corn stalks and fragrant roses.

Soil Sampler

Ages 7 and up

This craft will create a colorful sample of the different types of soil found in the earth's crust. By placing seeds in the sampler you will learn what types of plants can be grown in different types of soil. As your Soil Sampler grows, the vibrant colors of red, blue, green, and other earthy tones will decorate a windowsill.

Materials

Clear glass vase or large glass jar
5 stones, varied colors
10 dried beans
Small package red modeling clay
½ cup sand
½ cup potting soil
Handful grass seed
1 cup water
5 drops blue food coloring (optional)
Spoon

1. Put the five stones in the bottom of the vase.

2. Put one or two beans among the stones. Put the modeling clay on top of the stones.

3. Push the clay down upon the stones so that the clay has a flat top. Be sure to leave a little pocket of air at the bottom between the rocks.

4. Push two beans into the clay near the glass so that you can see the beans.

5. Add the sand and a few more beans.

6. Pack the sand down tight (but not so tight that the air pocket around the rock is closed up). Once again, check to make sure that the beans are close enough to the sides of the glass so that you can see them.

7. Now add the soil and the remaining beans, again close to the glass.

8. Sprinkle the grass seed on top.

9. Put the blue food coloring in your cup of water and mix with a spoon. This step is optional. But the blue food coloring makes it easier to watch how the water is absorbed by the different kinds of soil and the roots of the plants.

10. Slowly add a little bit of the water to your vase, enough to make the topsoil wet. Watch the water slowly work its way down through the vase. Did it make it through the clay to the rocks? If so, how long did it take?

11. Set your vase in a sunny spot and add more blue water each week. Don't over water, because too much water harms many plants. Stop if a puddle forms. Watch to see if your beans and grass grow and in which layer of soil in your Soil Sampler they grew best—clay, sand, or topsoil.

Sponge Tracks

Ages 6 and under

The dirt on the ground tells many stories, including which animals are lurking nearby. Tracks in the dirt tell us a lot about our surroundings, such as whether a bear or bunny has passed through the area, or which direction to go if we're looking for deer. Making Sponge Tracks is the art of animals painted in dirt.

Materials

4 or more small cleaning sponges

Black marker

Scissors

Old newspaper

Light-colored construction paper or watercolor
    paper, any size

Bowl of dirt

1 cup water

Spoon

1. Draw different animal-track shapes on your sponges with the black marker. You can make up the shapes or look up tracks in an animal book. Make these large enough to leave a big impression on your paper. Go to www.bear-tracker.com/mammals.html for tracks of some animals.
2. Cut out the track shapes with your scissors.
3. Place your construction or watercolor paper on top of the newspaper.

4. Pour a little water in the dirt and mix well until mud forms.
5. Dip your sponges in the mud and press them onto the paper. Crisscross your Sponge Tracks so that your final work of art looks like a bunch of wild animals have just walked this way and that way all over your paper!

Clay Beads

Ages 6 and under

As we have learned, Native Americans first used clay to make pottery, jewelry, and art. Because clay is strong, it is a great material for many things. Clay has been used in building, too. Clay is formed into bricks or tiles and then baked until it becomes hard and waterproof. Clay bricks and tiles can be used to create homes or buildings. Clay is mixed with crushed rock to make cement, which is used in construction and poured into concrete sidewalks for us to walk on.

Clay can also be beautiful to wear. This craft is a simple way to make Clay Beads or a clay pin from nature, adding some texture with sand.

Materials

Small spade

Bucket

3 sheets old newspaper

Cookie sheet or cutting board

1 piece aluminum foil to cover cookie sheet, 24 × 12 inches

Water

Ball of clay, about the size of your fist

3 toothpicks

1 cup plain or colored sand

Safety pin

Acrylic paints (optional)

Paintbrush (optional)

🍂 *Nature Notes*

Going on a Clay Hunt

Clay is made up of many things, such as carbon, iron, and copper. These chemical elements give clay its different colors, such as black, blue, and red. Clay can be found all over the world, but some areas tend to have more clay than others. Geologists who study rocks and minerals help us to learn about areas rich with clay. Another way that we know an area has clay nearby is by all the ancient pottery found by archeologists. Archeologists are scientists who help us to learn about history by uncovering artifacts (objects from the human past). Archeologists have found many clay objects made by the Pueblo Indians living in the Southwest; along the eastern coast made by various Woodland Indian tribes; and also in the Northeast, where the Iroquois once thrived. But clay can also be found in many other parts of the world, such as China, Africa, Mexico, and even in your own backyard! Sometimes if you dig deep enough under the dirt, you'll find a lot of hard clay in the soil. You can tell when your soil has clay particles by squeezing it in your fist and seeing if it forms a heavy lump.

If you don't live in an area where clay can be found easily, you can make your own pretend salt clay. See the recipe on page 99.

1. Take your spade and bucket and go in search of a clay bed. If it is winter or you cannot find clay, you can use the homemade salt clay recipe (see page 99) or buy some air-dry modeling clay from a craft store.

2. Cover your table or workspace with the newspaper.

3. Cover the cookie sheet or board with the aluminum foil and set aside.

4. Take your clay and form a tight ball. If the clay is hard, you may need to add some water to make it easier to work with.

5. Slam the clay ball onto your work surface to get rid of any air bubbles inside so that your clay will not break when it dries. Be sure to roll and knead the clay between your hands so that it becomes soft and easy to use.

6. Begin with a small piece of clay. Roll it between your fingers until it forms a ball.

7. Poke a hole through the center of the ball with your toothpick. Now you have your first bead that can be strung on a bracelet, necklace, shoelace, or hair ribbon.

8. Hold the ball between your fingers. Use the toothpick to draw designs on your bead, creating stripes, dots, or a drawing of an animal.

9. When you are done, gently roll the bead in some loose sand sprinkled on the newspaper. This will make the bead glisten in the sunlight. Continue to make beads until you have enough for your jewelry. Place all the beads on the aluminum-covered board to dry.

10. Make a matching pin by pulling a larger piece of clay and rolling it into a ball.

11. Press this ball flat with your thumb. Then press the safety pin into one side of the flat circle. Be sure that the pin is big enough to fit almost the entire length of the flattened circle so that it will not be too heavy to wear.

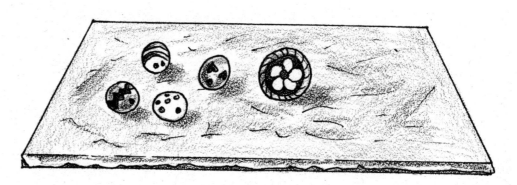

12. Turn the flattened circle over. Create a design on the front with the toothpick.
13. Place your clay pin on the cookie sheet. Let dry overnight or in the sun. When completely dry, it is ready to wear.
14. You can also paint your Clay Beads with acrylic paints and a small paintbrush.

Sunrise

Ages 7 and up

The sun is a very important part of our environment. It is necessary for life on earth, giving everything light and warmth to live and grow. Our earth revolves around the sun. Where it is in its cycle determines the different seasons. Over the years, many have celebrated the magic of the sun in paintings, drawings, and sculptures. This craft is another three-dimensional work of art that also celebrates the wonder of our sun. When complete you will see a picture of a Sunrise. As you get closer you'll see the sun bursting from its frame.

Materials

Paper lunch sack

Scissors

Old picture frame, no larger than 7 × 7 inches

Pencil

3 sheets old newspaper

Clay ball, size of your hand

Plastic knife

Gold-colored paint

Paintbrush, ¼ inch wide

1. With the scissors, cut open the paper lunch sack along the foldable creases on the sides. When finished you will have a flat piece of brown paper.
2. Place the picture frame on top of the bag. Trace around the outside of the frame with the pencil.
3. Cut out the brown paper along the lines you traced.
4. Crumple the brown paper into a ball and then smooth it out.
5. Place the paper inside the frame. This will be the background of the picture.
6. Put the newspapers on your table or workspace.
7. Pull a piece from the clay. Roll it into a ball about 2 inches in diameter.
8. Press it flat while rotating your palm until it forms the shape of a circle.

9. Cut the circle in half with the knife. Put one half on the bottom center of your picture.

10. Take the remaining piece of clay and break into 20 pieces.

11. Roll each piece until it forms a long tube like a pretzel stick.

12. Firmly press each of these atop your sun, spaced and sticking out in all directions. Let dry. Be sure to attach the bottom, or end, of each piece of clay to the sun. Your sun now has its rays.

13. When the clay is dry, paint every other ray with the gold paint. Also paint the body of the sun. Let dry. Your Sunrise will be a star!

Hiking Heart

Ages 6 and under

Hiking is good for your heart! Walking up hills, across meadows, or even through the city helps you stay fit and healthy. The heart is a very important part of your body. It works hard to pump the blood through your body. The blood it pumps carries oxygen and other nutrients through your body. We need healthy hearts to live. That means taking good care of this muscle by eating a well-balanced diet with plenty of fruits and vegetables, and getting plenty of exercise. Ask a friend or a family member to go on a hike with you. When you return, make this Hiking Heart craft together to remember the day you shared.

Materials

1 big block air-dry clay, or 2–3 cups clay from the ground or salt clay (see page 99 for the recipe)
2 sheets waxed paper, 20 × 20 inches
Rolling pin

Plastic knife

Collection of small items that you find on your hike, such as a shell, pebble, leaf, bottle cap, or even a penny

Pencil or toothpick

1. Place the clay on top of the waxed paper. Cover with another piece of waxed paper.
2. Using the rolling pin, roll out the clay until it is about 1/2 inch thick and at least 10 inches wide around. The waxed paper on top of the clay will prevent it from sticking to the rolling pin.
3. With the pencil, trace the shape of a heart along the outer edge of your clay.
4. Using the plastic knife, cut off the excess clay so that your flattened piece is in the shape of a heart.
5. Each person on the hike should gently but firmly press a hand in the clay heart to leave an impression. The person with the biggest hand should go first. It is fine if the impressions overlap, just as long as you can see part of the hand shape of everyone who went on the hike.
6. Take the items you found on your walk and press them into the clay inside of your handprints.

7. Using the pencil or toothpick, sign your names and place the date somewhere on the clay heart.
8. Put your clay outside or in a warm place to dry. When it is completely dry, you'll have made a Hiking Heart that shares with everyone the special things you found on your hike and the special friends who went with you.

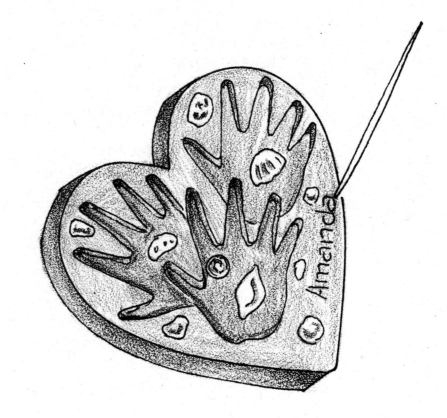

Sand Glass

Have you ever heard of sand glass, sea glass, beach glass, mermaid's tears, or fulgurites (FULL-guh-rites)? All of these are names for glass that is shaped and made by nature. *Sea glass* includes the little gems of color that wash ashore and sparkle in the sun. Sea glass comes in colors such as white, green, brown, and blue, but the colors that are harder to find are oranges and reds. Sea glass begins as a bottle or piece of glass accidentally tossed into the ocean from a ship or dragged into the ocean on a shoreline. The glass is broken by the sea, tumbled by waves, and polished by many grains of sand until it's smooth like a stone and sparkles in the sun. Another form of glass is created when lightning or a meteorite strikes sandy soil. When lightning hits the sandy soil, all the air and water in the area of sand instantly heats up and fuses the sand particles together. They form a glass called a fulgurite.

Glittering Sand Castle

Ages 7 and up

Have you ever played on the beach and built a sand castle? Soon the waves rush the shore and knock it all down. Waves are caused by wind and changes in the tide—the rise and fall of the ocean's surface caused by the gravitational pull of the moon and the sun upon the earth as they move faster or slower toward one another. Low tide happens when the water is pulled away from the shore. High tide happens when the water moves up farther onto the shore.

This craft builds a Glittering Sand Castle that sparkles in the sun and doesn't wash away after high tide. This is a project that will take some time to create, but anyone who can use glue can make a beautiful palace fit for a king or queen.

Materials

1 piece thick cardboard, $8\frac{1}{2} \times 11$ inches
1 large sheet aluminum foil, big enough to cover the
    cardboard

Collection of small cardboard boxes, about 3–7 inches in height, such as jewelry boxes, juice boxes, or food containers

Bucket of sand

Plastic tub or bowl

Aluminum foil and leftover colorful wrapping paper cut into small pieces, or package of silver and gold glitter (optional)

Spoon

Rubber gloves

2 cardboard toilet-tissue tubes

Craft glue or homemade Natural Glue, p. xiv

2 paper cones from an iced Sno-Cone, or you can use two small paper cups

2 smaller pieces aluminum foil, about 5 × 7 inches

Rubber cement

5 sheets blue tissue paper

Rag

1. Cover the cardboard with the aluminum foil. Set down on a flat surface or worktable.

2. Arrange and stack the boxes in any design you wish to make the main body of the castle. Do not glue anything down yet.

3. Pour some of the sand in the tub or bowl.

4. Sprinkle in cut-up aluminum foil and wrapping paper or some gold and silver glitter. Mix well with the spoon.

5. Put on the rubber gloves.

6. Cover the tissue tubes in glue, spreading it evenly with your fingers.

7. Roll the tubes in the sand-sparkle mixture. Let dry.

8. Do the same with all of your cardboard boxes. Rub them with glue and roll them in the sand-sparkle mixture.

9. Let all pieces dry completely.

10. Cover the two paper cones or paper cups with the smaller pieces of aluminum foil. Turn them upside down over the cardboard tissue tubes.

11. Glue these together by putting glue around one edge of the tubes. Put them back inside the cones and let dry.

12. Put all of the boxes and cone-covered tissue tubes back in place to form a castle. Stand back and see whether you're happy with the way your castle looks. Make any changes now *before* you glue everything in place.

13. When you have a castle shape that you like, put rubber cement on the bottom of the boxes and cement them in place one by one. Let dry completely. When your castle is done, it will need a moat filled with water.

14. Take your blue tissue paper and rip into strips.

15. Crinkle up the strips, then press flat.

16. Glue down the tissue strips in a circle around your castle. The shine from the aluminum foil will make your water sparkle. You can also add other decorations to your castle, such as flowers, sequins, cattails, or whatever you find that will make your Glittering Sand Castle special.

Sea Sparkler

Ages 6 and under

When the sun reflects on the ocean's surface, a sparkling world appears. Underneath the surface of the water the sun's rays capture the colors of all the plant and animal life in the sea, such as silky and slimy seaweed, bright orange and green coral, sparkling silver needlefish, brilliant blue parrotfish. A Sea Sparkler shows that water and sunlight together can create a magical world whether you are near the ocean or not.

Materials

3 sheets old newspaper

$1/2$ cup sand

$1/4$ cup aluminum foil cut into tiny pieces, or glitter (optional)

Bowl

1 sheet waxed paper, 10 × 10 inches

1 sheet light-blue construction paper, $8^1/2$ × 11 inches

Water-based paints of greens and blues

Soap and water

Rag

Craft glue or homemade Natural Glue, p. xiv

1. Spread the newspapers on your table or workspace.
2. Place the sand and aluminum foil pieces or glitter in the bowl and mix well. Set aside.

3. Set the construction paper and waxed paper on the newspaper.

4. Pour a little of the blue and green paint on the waxed paper. Place your hand flat in one of the paints so that it covers your handprint.

5. Along the bottom of your construction paper, stamp several of your handprints using different shades of blue and green. You are making the seaweed and corals that cover the seafloor, so press your hands down straight, then to the left, then to the right, to represent the way seaweed moves from the ocean waves. Wash your hands with soap and water. You'll need the rag to help scrub them.

6. Now you can add your fish. With the glue, draw the shapes of fish all over your sea scene. You can make big fins, eyes, or any design you want.

7. Sprinkle the sparkle-sand all over the glue. Let dry.

8. Turn your paper sideways and let the extra sparkle-sand fall away onto the newspaper.

9. Add a few more drops of glue coming from the fishes' mouths just like bubbles would sparkle under the sea. Sprinkle sparkle-sand. Let dry. Then shake off as above, and enjoy your Sea Sparkler.

Sandman

Ages 7 and up

Sand is made up of rock broken down into tiny pieces. Sand is also made of small pieces of coral, shell, lava, and other things, such as quartz and black stone. Because these are so colorful, sand is, too, when you look closely. The sand made from well-worn rocks and stone gives deserts their warm tan and earthy tones. The white beaches found on tropical islands are made up of sand that comes from coral and shells. All colors and types of sand can be used in many different crafts and works of art. This craft creates a funny little Sandman you can use as a puppet or doll. It is heavy enough to be a bookend or paperweight. You can keep him out all year long, although he looks a lot like his brother, the snowman.

Materials

1 empty Pom bottle (Pom, a pomegranate juice, can be found in the grocery store) or a tall glass jelly jar

Funnel

3 cups white or light-colored sand

1 Styrofoam ball or sheet old newspaper crunched in a ball, 3–4 inches in size

1 piece black construction paper, tissue, or felt cut into an 8-inch strip

Craft glue or homemade Natural Glue, p. xiv

2 buttons or wiggle eyes (found in craft stores)

4 pebbles, very small

1. Place the funnel into the top of the Pom bottle or jelly jar.

2. Completely fill the bottle with sand.

3. Take the Styrofoam ball or newspaper ball and gently push it on the top of the bottle.

4. Place your black paper or felt around the neck of the bottle, under the Styrofoam or newspaper ball. This is the scarf.

5. Place a few drops of glue on the scarf where it touches the bottle so that it will stay in place.

6. Glue the two wiggle eyes or buttons on the Sandman's head. Gently push the pebbles into the Styrofoam ball in the shape of a mouth. If you need, add glue to the back of the pebbles or buttons. Now your Sandman is ready to watch out for winter or summer!

Messy Mats

Ages 6 and under

Mud and clay may be messy, but they're useful to many people. Many things stick to or get stuck in wet clay. That is why we can find fossils in clay buried for thousand or even millions of years. Wet clay and mud can help to heal and clean our skin. Many doctors encourage people to take healing mud baths or to use wet clay masks on their skin to clear away dirt and oil, and give skin a smooth texture. Wet clay and mud can be beautiful, too. Artists use wet clay to seal up holes in pottery before it is baked. This kind of wet clay is called *slip.* People have used it for centuries to make smooth, strong, sturdy pieces of pottery and art. As an earth artist, you can use wet clay and mud to make a Messy Mat. The mat in a picture is the paper frame that runs along the inside of the metal or wood frame. A picture framed in earth art will add so much to what people see. It adds another piece of art to what someone is already looking at and might even steal the show. Messy Mats are fun to make, quick to bake, and easy to decorate!

Materials

1 picture frame with a light-colored mat board, any size

1 brown paper grocery bag

Pencil

Scissors

2 sheets old newspaper

Rubber gloves

1 cup water

1 cup dirt in a bowl

1 cup clay, found outside or from a craft store, in a bowl

Spoon

1 cup sand

Mod Podge, gloss finish (available at craft stores)

1 small cup

1 paintbrush, 2 inches wide

Photograph or drawing that is small enough to fit inside the frame

A small piece of masking tape

1. Carefully pull out the mat board from the picture frame. Put it on top of the grocery bag.
2. Use the pencil to trace around the outside of the mat board onto the grocery bag.
3. Cut the traced square on the grocery bag.
4. Crumple up this grocery bag square. Set it aside.
5. Set your mat board on top of the newspapers.
6. Put on your rubber gloves.
7. Pour about $\frac{1}{4}$ cup of water into the bowl of dirt and mix thoroughly. Pour another $\frac{1}{4}$ cup of water into the bowl of clay and mix thoroughly.

8. With your hands, scoop out some of the moist dirt and rub it on the mat board. Then do the same with the wet clay. Make sure that you cover the board. It's great, too, if you end up with chunks of dirt and clay on it. This gives it texture, something you can feel.
9. When the mat is covered, carefully rub in some sand.
10. Place your mat in the sun or a warm spot to bake dry.
11. When it is dry, pour a little of Plaid's Mod Podge in a cup. Use the paintbrush to cover the Messy Mat. (Mod Podge is a milky white liquid that dries transparent in less than 10 minutes.) Let dry. It's OK if you get dirt on the brush and into the Mod Podge. Remember, you're adding texture.
12. Smooth out the grocery bag square and set your photograph or drawing in the middle. Put a small piece of tape behind the photo or drawing it to hold it centered on the grocery bag. Center the Messy Mat on top for your border.
13. Put everything back in the picture frame and hang it up.

Save the Beach

Many of the coastlines around the world are changing. Areas that were once covered with sandy beaches are now covered with buildings or have disappeared, washed underneath the ocean. This type of washing away of beaches is called erosion. As the waves move up farther on a beach at high tide, sand is slowly dragged back into the water and travels someplace else. Sometimes the sand is moved farther down the beach; sometimes it moves to another place far away from the shore. In the long term, the sea level will continue to rise in many areas, swallowing up the sand. This happens because the ice at the North and South Poles is melting. Population and industry growth lead to an increased release of gases that warm our environment, affect the ultraviolet light–protective cloud covering over our planet (called the ozone layer), and contribute to the melting of the ice. The burning of fossil fuels, fumes from cars, and lighting of big cities contributes to global warming. Fossil fuels are fossil-based materials removed from inside the earth that are used for fuel energy, such as oil and coal.

People, nonprofit organizations, and the government, including the National Oceanic and Atmospheric Association (www.noaa.gov), the Cousteau Society (www.cousteau.org/en), and the United Nations Educational, Scientific and Cultural Organization (www.unesco.org/en) are working together to help save the beaches. One way to do this is to limit the amount of energy we use to slow the effects of global warming. Turning off lights, reusing materials, keeping the beaches free of litter and garbage (you'll learn more about recycling in chapter 6), and carpooling are all ways to save energy and protect nature. Government offices, such as the Office of Ocean and Coastal Resource Management (http://coastalmanagement.noaa.gov) and the National Park Service (www.nps.gov), have been actively pushing for new buildings to be set farther back from eroding shores and to limit new construction on sandy beaches. They promote "beach nourishment" by putting more sand on the beach to rebuild the sandy coastlines. One project, called Planning for Coastline Change, by the United Nations Educational, Scientific and Cultural Organization, or UNESCO, includes work with small islands to predict the possible changes that may occur to the shoreline if too much construction occurs nearby. Although sandy beaches are great places to stay or live, it is important to protect them so they'll be there for years to come.

4
Plants, Grasses, and Seeds

Plants come in all shapes, colors, and sizes. Trees are a very big type of plant. This chapter will focus on smaller plants, such as those that produce flowers or cover the ground, such as grasses. We will also discuss seeds—the very small beginnings of every plant. Not all plants are green and leafy. Mushrooms and toadstools are brown and gray. Cacti have needles. Some plants are big and bushy, such as dogwood or holly. Others, such as mosses, are tiny and flat and stay close to the ground. Wherever you look outside, you're likely to see hundreds of different types of plants. Can you name all the plants you see? Getting to know plants and grasses is not only fun, it's smart, too, because not all plants are friendly. It's always a good idea to know whether a plant is safe to touch or eat.

Chinaberry and bittersweet are two plants that produce beautiful, brightly colored berries that are often used for decorating. Some parts of these plants are used in medicines, candles, paints, or soaps, but their berries are poisonous and can be very harmful if eaten. Use your nature journal or a notebook to draw pictures of the plants you find on your nature walks. Before you begin, you may want to look at the following books to help you better understand the world of plants:

Plant by Fleur Star. New York: DK, 2005. (Ages 4–8)

Plants We Know by O. Irene Sevrey Miner. Chicago: Children's Press, 1981. (Ages 5–9).

What Plant Is This? by Marcia S. Freeman. Vero Beach, FL: Rourke, 2005. (Ages 9–12)

Once you have sketched a picture and made some notes about a plant that you find in nature, ask a teacher, librarian, or some other adult to help you look it up in an encyclopedia, such as the *American Horticultural Society Encyclopedia of Plants and Flowers*. New York: DK, 2002.

Potpourri

Ages 7 and up

Wouldn't it be nice to bring the fresh fragrance of flowers and plants home with you to enjoy all year long? During the late summer, when flowers and fruits are blooming in gardens and at fruit stands, potpourri is often made to capture the smells and sights of summer. Potpourri is a mixture of spices, dried flowers, and fruits. It can fill a room with a healthy, fresh fragrance. And it's safer for us to breathe and for our environment than canned air sprays.

Materials

Small bowl filled with scented flowers, such as roses, violets, lavender, geraniums, and marigolds.

Cookie sheet

1 cup uniodized salt (available at craft stores and some grocers)*

2 paper towel sheets

1 piece cardboard, $8^1/_2 \times 11$ inches

1 lemon, 1 orange, and 1 apple, thinly sliced

Medium-sized bowl

$^1/_2$ cup mixed spices, such as cinnamon, nutmeg, and cloves

*Uniodized or noniodized salt is salt that doesn't have iodine added. It is sometimes called sea salt, pickling salt, or natural salt. It can be found alongside regular table salt at many grocers.

1. Gently pull all the petals and leaves off the fresh flowers and place them flat on the cookie sheet.
2. Put the cookie sheet out of direct sunlight. Let the fresh flowers dry.
3. About a day after they begin to dry, sprinkle the cup of uniodized salt on top.
4. Put the two paper towel sheets on the piece of cardboard. Spread the lemon, orange, and apple slices over them.

5. Put this cardboard tray in the sunlight to dry. This may take several sunny days.

6. When the fruit has dried, put it in the bowl. When the flowers have dried, gently shake off the salt, and add the petals and leaves to the bowl of fruit.

7. Add in the spices.

8. Using your hands, gently mix everything together. You can keep your Potpourri in this bowl and enjoy the scents all winter long.

Mushroom Magic

Ages 6 and under

Mushrooms and toadstools are a type of fungus that is part of the plant family. If you pick up a mushroom, underneath you'll find many fleshy little lines called *gills*. The gills help the mushroom or toadstool to send out tons of little spores into the environment. These spores can turn into new mushrooms. They will also turn into art in Mushroom Magic.

Materials

Gardening gloves

Bag for gathering mushrooms and toadstools

Book on mushrooms and toadstools*

3 sheets old newspaper

1 sheet waxed paper, 24 × 12 inches

1 black or dark-colored piece construction paper or foam board

Glow-in-the-dark paint, available at craft stores, or nail polish

5–6 toadstool or mushroom caps

5 plastic bowls

1 can non-aerosol hairspray or artist's fixative spray (available at craft stores)

Good Mushrooms and Bad Toadstools by Allan Fowler. New York: Children's Press, 1998. (Ages 4–8)

1. Put on your gardening gloves. Gather the mushroom or toadstool caps. Be sure to use your book to identify which mushrooms are safe to pick. You may also use store-bought mushrooms that have large heads or caps, such as portabellas.

2. Spread out the newspaper sheets on a table or work surface. Put the sheet of waxed paper on top of the newspaper. Put the dark paper or foam board next to the waxed paper.

3. Pour some of the glow-in-the-dark paint or nail polish on the waxed paper. If you are using nail polish, keep a window open.

4. Take one of your mushrooms or toadstools and gently pull off the stem. Do this slowly so that the head, or cap, does not tear or break. Gently press the cap into the paint or nail polish to act as a sponge. Then put it on the dark paper like a stamp. Do this a few times, but leave space for the other mushroom cap designs.

5. When you are finished, gently lay the other caps on the spaces remaining on the dark paper.

6. Cover the mushroom caps with the bowls. Wait several hours or overnight.

7. When you remove the bowls and caps, you will discover that the caps have released their spores onto the paper in a cool-looking design.

8. Spray the picture with the hairspray or artist's spray to keep the spores in place. Don't get too close while spraying. When the spray dries, you can admire your Mushroom Magic in the light or in the dark.

Plant Painting

Ages 7 and up

It's hard to imagine a world without paint. Just about every store you go to has some type of paint available for sale—paint for houses, paint for artists, and paints that are used in school. Paint hasn't always been around, but color certainly has. Since prehistoric times, people have used plants to color their world. Scientists have discovered that different types of plants were used to create colorful cave drawings. In fact, some plants provide such a strong color that they are still used today in manufacturing paints. An example is the blue from indigo. An easy way to begin to experiment with paints made from things in the natural world is to create a plant painting. This craft will teach you how to mix plants with a base, such as mud, to create different colors. If you want, you can store leftover Plant Paints in small containers, such as baby food jars, to use

All the Colors of the Earth

Thousands of years ago, before there were craft stores and manufactured paints, people looked to the earth for their craft materials. Art on cave walls and colorful masks and clothing were decorated with paints made from crushed seeds, plants, water, oils, and dirt. Nature provides us with many tools for making art, and today the earth still provides us with materials to create paints.

Nature's paints come in all the colors of the earth and every shade you can imagine. You just need to know where to look. You'll find the color for your paints and dyes from clay, fruits, and vegetables. Below is a list of nature paints and the colors each creates. (Warning: When picking materials from the earth for paints and dyes, never put anything you find into your mouth. Many berries and plants, although bright and friendly in color, can be poisonous to animals and people. Be sure you wash your hands completely, with soap and warm water, after picking plants and berries. Keep all of your unused items stored in your earth art kit, away from pets and younger brothers and sisters.)

Nature's Paint

Color	*Nature's Paint*
Red	Crushed beets
	Cranberries
	Dogwood bark
Yellow and Gold	Onionskins
	Goldenrod stems
	Marigold petals
	Crushed dandelion flowers
Black	Crushed charcoal
	Hickory bark
Blue	Sunflower seeds
	Alfalfa flowers
	Indigo leaves

1. To prepare colors from plant leaves and bark, you have to soak the plant skins, leaves, seeds, flowers, or bark in very hot water overnight or even for several days. Cranberries and beets should be peeled and cut up into small pieces, then boiled in hot water for color. Please ask an adult to help you. Never heat water or use a knife by yourself!

2. Use the colored water that is left over for your Nature's Paints. Colored water can be stored in a baby food or jelly jar for up to a month.

3. When using charcoal, crush the piece of charcoal with a rock or by using your foot. The small pieces can be stored in a jar to use in plant painting.

Remember to add new colors and ingredients to your Nature's Paints as you discover them. As you learn and explore more about nature, you will also learn new ways of using nature to make art and crafts.

later. If your paints become dry, just add a little more water and mix well.

Adult supervision required

Materials

Scoop of dirt or clay, about the size of your fist

Metal spoon with strong handle

1 cup water

Several small sturdy cups, one for each color of paint you make (glass, ceramic, or heavy plastic cups work best)

Nature's Paints, 1 cup ingredients for each different color you choose (for example, 1 cup cranberries to make red paint)

1 sheet paper, $8\frac{1}{2} \times 11$ inches

Paintbrush

1. Using your metal spoon, collect some dirt or clay, about the size of your fist, and put it into one of your nature paint containers.
2. Pour in half of the cup of water and blend until the mixture turns into smooth mud. You may need to add more water until the mixture is smooth like thick paint. This will be the base for your paints. Now you need to add color.

3. Using your spoon, put a little bit of mud in another cup. Add one of your Nature's Paint colors, such as the colored water from the cranberries. Start with $\frac{1}{4}$ cup of your Nature's Paint ingredients. Slowly add more if you want the color brighter. Stir the mixture until all of the Nature's Paint ingredients are blended. Mix well. If necessary, add a little more water so that your paint is smooth.

4. After you have mixed all the colors you want, use your paintbrush to create a painting on your paper. You may want to draw a picture of a tree or a colorful bouquet of flowers. Perhaps you will choose to use charcoal-colored paint and draw a penguin or zebra. Your painting will not only have the most amazing colors, but when

the mud-based paints dry, it will have a unique texture.

Be sure to let your Plant Painting dry completely before you hang it up on the wall.

Earth Dye T-Shirt

Ages 6 and under

Plants have been used not only to create paints, but also to create dyes to color fabrics and other items. Native Americans, Europeans, and early American pioneers all used plants to dye skins, fabric, wool, and thread for sewing. Although mixing and matching plants could create every color of the rainbow, some colors were easier to create than others. Browns, reds, and yellows were more common because many plants, when boiled, will turn these shades. But purples and blues, especially bright colors, were often harder and more time-consuming to create, so fabrics and threads made from these plants had more value. You can experiment with dyes and see what colors are easy to make from the plants you find where you live. Then you can show off the colors of the earth by wearing them on a T-shirt. Now that you know what colors different plants and vegetables make, you can put them together to make a colorful Earth Dye T-Shirt.

Adult supervision required

Materials

5 sheets old newspaper

Spoon

3 small containers, such as plastic cups or baby food jars

Collection of berries and flowers for dye colors (see Plant Painting activity above)

Water

Plastic tub or cookie sheet

1 cotton T-shirt, white

10 or more rubber bands

Rubber gloves

1. Cover your workspace or tabletop with a few sheets of newspaper.

2. Line your tub or cookie sheet with the remaining newspapers. Set it on top of the newspaper covering your workspace.

3. Grab a section of your T-shirt and squeeze your hand around it in a fist. Put a rubber band around the T-shirt section at the base of your fist. Do this all over your T-shirt so that it looks like it has a bunch of puffy cloth sections sticking out of rubber bands. Some sections of the shirt can have two sets of rubber bands for double color. (See below for instructions on how to make double colors.)

4. Put on your rubber gloves. Prepare several containers filled with different dye colors. Follow the directions on page 70 for Nature's Paints.

5. One at a time, slowly put each rubber-banded section of your T-shirt into a jar of color. Hold it there for a few minutes until you see the T-shirt turn color. Then remove it and let it dry. Meanwhile, put place another section of your T-shirt in the color. You can use several different colors if you like!

6. For the sections that have a double rubber band, you can double dip the tip of that section into a different color. This will create a new color. Red and yellow will make orange; blue and yellow will make green; blue and red will make purple. A mixture of many colors will make a brown or black. What other colors can you make?

7. When you are done dipping, put your T-shirt in the newspaper-lined tub or on a cookie sheet. Do not remove the rubber bands yet.

8. Using the spoon, carefully pour a little more of the dye colors on sections of the rubber-banded T-shirt. If you put the same color dye over the same color, it will make the color brighter. But if you mix colors, a new color will appear. You can mix and match your colors any way you like.

9. Let your T-shirt dry for at least 5 hours before removing the rubber bands. Then spread it flat to dry overnight before wearing.

10. Don't forget to hand wash your shirt or wash it separately in the washing machine. Otherwise your colors may bleed onto other clothing. In addition, always wash your Earth Dye T-Shirt in cold water to keep the colors from fading.

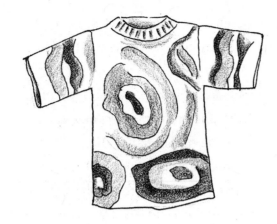

Color and Print Eggs

Ages 7 and up

Eggs can be colored with many different colors by boiling them in hot water along with various plants and vegetables. For example, if you want to color your egg gold, you can boil it with yellow onionskins. If you would like to dye your egg red, cut up a beet and put it in the pot instead. Dark leafy greens, such as spinach, will make your egg appear a green color when they are boiled together. (Remember: Never boil water without an adult's supervision.) There are many possibilities for your Color and Print Eggs.

Adult supervision required

Materials

12 eggs

Needle

Bowl

Towel

Cooking pot filled with water

One onion peeled, small carrots cut up, or a can of red beets

Scissors

3 printed paper napkins

Comic strips from newspapers

Handful leaves

Handful grasses

Craft glue or homemade Natural Glue, p. xiv

1 small bowl water

Rag

1. You can decorate your eggs hardboiled or you can empty the shells first. If you want to use napkin and comic book design decorations, it is best to use an eggshell that has been blown empty. An eggshell that has been blown empty no longer contains the liquids inside. An adult can help you by poking a hole in both ends of the eggshell with a needle and blowing the

inside of the egg into a bowl. Save the inside of the eggs for cooking or other craft projects.

2. Wash the eggshell thoroughly and carefully by holding it under running water. Let it dry on a towel.

3. You can color the empty shell in water using nature's own colors. Boil the water with the onionskins, red beets, or carrots, depending on which color you would like. Once the water has turned color, remove pot from heat. Put the empty eggshell in the hot water and let it soak for at least an hour.

   If you want to color hardboiled eggs, put your egg inside the pot of water along with the nature colors you've chosen. Boil them together. The egg will naturally turn the color you choose. Let the egg dry well by placing it on top of a towel and setting it in a warm or sunny spot.

4. Cut out a design from a printed napkin or comic strip. You can also use grasses or leaves for your print if you want the eggs to look more natural.

5. Put plenty of glue on the back of the item you want to stick to the egg.

6. Press the print pattern, leaf, or grass onto the egg and smooth it down. Any excess glue should be picked up with your fingers and gently

smeared back over the design. A bit of water may make the glue press more smoothly.

7. Continue to smooth your fingers over the picture until it sticks. Let dry overnight. When you are finished, the Color and Print Eggs should be displayed in a basket or bowl. Or, if you wish, string the empty shells and hang them on a tree.

Greenhouse Goodness!

An *ecosystem* is a part of nature that can function by itself, creating its own water, food, and air. A small window box filled with different types of plants and insects is an ecosystem. So is a greenhouse, made of glass, with a lot of plants inside. In the 1700s, families in many northern countries built greenhouses to protect and grow warm-weather plants all year long. These greenhouses made their homes more beautiful and inviting. Sitting in a warm room filled with bright green and colorful plants and flowers made the cold winters and rainy seasons seem less harsh. Many greenhouses were used to grow orange and lemon trees. Greenhouses of this kind are called orangeries. They were very popular because they allowed people to have warm-weather fruits all year long. Greenhouses were not only an important source for fruits and beautiful plants. They were also a great place for learning and sharing knowledge of plant life. Soon local governments saw the importance of building large greenhouses for public use. These are called *conservatories*. Many are still open to the public today. The Phipps Conservatory and Botanical Gardens in Pittsburgh, Pennsylvania (www.phipps.conservatory.org), Chicago Botanic Gardens in Glencoe, Illinois (www.chicagobotanic.org), Garfield Park Conservatory, Chicago, Illinois (www.garfield-conservatory.org), Huntington Botanical Gardens in San Marino, California (www.huntington.org), and the United States Botanic Garden in Washington, DC (www.usbg.gov), all host very large conservatories where people can view unique and rare plants from all over the world. Conservatories are great places to learn about plants, trees, and natural life no matter what the weather is like outside!

24-Hour Terrarium

Ages 7 and up

Much like a very small greenhouse, a *terrarium* is a tiny little garden that grows inside a jar or glass container. This tiny world is sometimes referred to as an ecosystem. A terrarium is special because it grows all year long, no matter what the weather is like. Even if it is raining, snowing, or very dry and hot outside, the terrarium will grow. A terrarium is also special because it is a living world of soil, plants, and sometimes insects and animals, all in a small container that you can keep in your bedroom or any room that has plenty of sunlight. But one of the best things about a terrarium is that it is a living, breathing, tiny world that you create all by yourself. This 24-Hour Terrarium will need sunlight for growth. Instead of the moon or stars to shine light on your ecosystem at night, your 24-Hour Terrarium will glow in the dark, lighting your garden at all hours of the day.

Materials

Clear glass container, such as a candy jar or
fishbowl with a large opening at the top (large
enough to fit your hand through)

1 drop dishwashing soap and water

Dry towel

Old newspaper

4–5 light colored stones that can easily fit through
the opening of the glass jar

Glow-in-the-dark paint or fingernail polish

4–5 pieces of charcoal or a handful of gravel,
pebbles, or marbles

1 piece nylon stocking or cheesecloth, large enough
to cover bottom of container

Bag potting soil

Slightly damp rag

Very small plants, such as a tiny fern, dwarf
creeping fig, polka dot plant, clover, inch plant,
or any small plant that will not grow larger than
your jar (available outside, purchased at a
nursery, or started by you with seeds)

4–6 glow-in-the-dark stickers, small

$\frac{1}{4}$ cup of water

1 piece clear plastic wrap, twice the size of the
opening of your jar

Large rubber band

1. Wash your glass container and dry it well. Open
the windows in your kitchen or bathroom, or go
outside so that the nail polish fumes will not
bother you.

2. Spread your newspaper on a flat surface and
paint your stones using the glow-in-the-dark
paint or nail polish. Paint one side of each stone.
Once the stones are dry, turn them over and
paint the other side. Do this until you've covered
the stones with two or three coats. When you
finish, let them dry for at least 24 hours before
continuing.

3. Put the charcoal or a handful of gravel, pebbles,
or marbles in the bottom of your glass container.

4. Put the nylon stocking or cheesecloth on top of
the charcoal. This nylon barrier will prevent the
soil from dropping to the bottom of the container
and mixing with the charcoal, clogging your
plants' drainage systems.

5. Now it is time to add the potting soil into your
container, on top of the nylon stocking. This will
create a soil bed for your plants. Make a nice
thick bed for your plants, but don't fill your
entire jar with soil. Fill your jar a quarter of the
way up. Usually 1–2 cups of soil is plenty. Carefully put the soil in the middle of the jar and
spread it around. This will prevent you from get-

ting soil on the sides of the glass container. (If you do, you can easily wipe it down with the damp rag.)

6. Using your fingers, dig little holes in the soil bed to place your plant roots or seeds. Very carefully put a plant inside each hole. Be sure to space the plants at least 2 inches apart. This may mean that you can only put one or two plants in your terrarium. But remember, they will grow and fill your terrarium with color.

7. Carefully add more soil. Press it down firmly around each plant to eliminate air pockets near the roots.

8. Put your painted stones inside your container.

9. Put your glow-in-the-dark stickers on the inside rim of your jar opening.

10. Add some water to the soil, but don't add too much. If your soil is already very moist, you won't need any water. Your soil is moist if it sticks together when you pinch some of it between your fingers.

11. Cover the opening of the container with a sheet of the clear plastic wrap. Secure it tightly with your rubber band. You may need an adult or a second set of hands to help you hold the plastic covering while you place your rubber band around the opening. Set your magical garden in a sunny spot like a windowsill or on a table near the sunlight. Now it's time to watch your 24-Hour Terrarium grow and glow in the dark. Remember, even when it's very cold and most of the plants and animals have gone underground to live, you can admire the beautiful green world that you have created yourself.

Sparkling Braided Baskets

Ages 7 and up

Baskets have been used for thousands of years to carry things from one place to another, store stuff, and even as baby beds. Baskets are often made from dried grasses and rushes. These grasses are special because they are strong and dry and do not wilt when removed from their roots. Making Sparkling Braided Baskets is a smart way to put art to use. When you have finished covering your basket, it will be sturdy enough to carry and store things. It will be pretty enough to display or give as a gift.

Materials

Spool silver or gold metallic ribbon

Scissors

40 or more pieces of thick grasses, such as ribbon, cord, or elephant grass, at least 20 inches in length (long enough to stretch around the width of your wire basket with at least 5–10 inches to spare). You may need to tie ends of the grasses together to make longer strips.

🦎 *Nature Notes*

Grass for Dinner

Grasses are an excellent resource for building materials. Thatched roofs, woven baskets, and even some clothing are made from grasses. Grasses also produce flowers. Grass flowers don't have brightly colored petals, as do roses or daisies, but they do have little tufts of soft seeds that blossom at their tops. We eat many of these grasses and their flowers everyday. Rice, oats, wheat, sugar, and corn are just some of the food products made from grassy plants. In fact, about half of the people in the world depend on rice for a major part of their everyday dinners. Animals also love to eat grass. Goats, sheep, and cows all graze on farms covered with green grass. Pigs, birds, and squirrels love the grass that grows into corn. Horses and donkeys eat a lot of oats. Pandas also eat a type of grass called bamboo. Bamboo is big, sturdy, and tall; sometimes it's called a tree, but bamboo is really a type of grass. Bamboo is used to make many things, such as bridges, furniture, wood floors, and musical instruments. All types of creatures and people look forward to grass for dinner!

Wire basket frame, found at local craft stores, or you can use a plastic fruit basket from the grocery store

1. Cut several lengths of ribbon into strips the same length as your grasses.
2. Braid together two pieces of grass and one ribbon. To braid the three strips, tie three ends together into a knot. Lay them flat in front of you so that you have three strips running toward you and the knot away from you. Cross the right strip over the center. Then cross the left strip over the new center-most grass. Pull them out to the sides so that the braid becomes tight. Repeat, crossing the right strip over the center, then the left over the center, until you reach the bottom. Tie a knot at the end to keep your braid in place. Repeat this step until you have at least 20 tightly braided strips.
3. Weave the sparkling braided strips over and under the wire frame of the basket.
4. When you finish threading each braided strip around the basket, tightly tie the two ends of the strip together. Repeat this step until the entire wire basket is covered with sparkling braided strips. You may also need to weave through the handle, if your Sparkling Braided Basket has one.

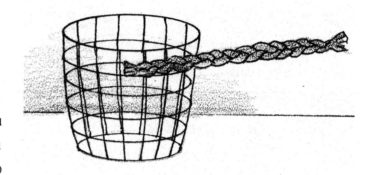

Grass Wraps

Ages 6 and under

Teaching others about our earth is a big part of what you are doing by making art and craft projects from earth materials. When you share some of your art as a gift, it shows that you care about this person and about the earth. Grass Wraps are a great way to share your artwork with everyone you know.

Materials

3–5 seed heads or flowers of grasses (These are the fluffy ends that pop up in the summer.)

Acrylic paint, Nature's Paints, p. 70, or Cornstarch Paint, p. xv

1 sheet construction paper or used office paper, any size

Mod Podge, matte (for a more natural look) or either gloss or sparkle (for a shine)–the choice is yours

Small plastic tub or jar

Small paintbrush

1 cup short grass

Several long strands ribbon grass or ornamental grass

1. Dip the heads of the grass into the acrylic paint. Gently press them all over the paper to make cool-looking imprints.
2. Let the paint dry.
3. Take your Mod Podge and pour a little into the tub or jar.
4. With the paintbrush, put the Mod Podge on the paper and glue on pieces of grass. Glue the grass in any design all over the paper. You can go in between the grass head prints or do a crosshatch design all over. Anything can be art!
5. Press the grass firmly in place. With the paintbrush, add more Mod Podge over the top of the grass to seal it to the paper. Let it dry completely.
6. When the paper, grass, and paint are completely dry, you can use it as gift wrap.
7. Instead of a bow, use the long ribbon grass or ornamental grass to tie up your Grass Wrap.

Natural Wind Sock

Ages 7 and up

Wind socks are used to determine the direction of the wind. The sock points in the same direction the wind is blowing. Wind socks are typically made out of fabrics and metals and can take some time to mold and sew. Here is an easy Natural Wind Sock made from natural materials. It works well and looks great when the wind begins to blow.

Materials

12 husks from corncobs (A husk is the green leafy part on the outside of the ear of corn. You'll get 3–5 husks from each ear of corn.)

4 plastic milk jug rings

Rubber cement

20 strands raffia or dried grasses, each at least 8 inches long

1 piece twine, 12 inches long

2 twigs

1. Start by attaching the ends of three corn husks to a plastic milk jug ring. Do so by putting rubber cement on an inch of the corn husk and wrapping it around the ring. You should space the husks evenly, making sure that there is at least 6 inches of husk hanging down.

2. In between each corn husk, tie one end of a piece of raffia or dried grass.

3. Take a new piece of raffia and wrap it around the loose ends of the cornhusks, raffia, or grass.

Tie the new piece of raffia in a knot. When you are done, all the loose ends of the husks, grass, and raffia will now be tied together by the raffia. Do this for all four rings of husks.

4. Using the twine, secure the two twigs together in the shape of a cross. To do so, lay one twig flat on your workspace so that the end points toward you. Lay another twig on top of it to make a cross. Pick up the twigs by pinching and holding them together at the point where they meet. Using a new piece of raffia, wrap it around the point where the twigs meet. Continue wrapping the raffia very tightly around and around in all directions, but do not tie your fingers to the twigs! When you have finished wrapping the twigs, they should hold together on their own. Tie a tight knot with the two loose ends of the raffia. The twig running side to side is your crossbar. The one running up and down is your post.

5. You'll need to wrap all the twine around the point where the two twigs meet. You may want to put a little of the rubber cement over this so that it will dry securely. Let it dry completely.

6. Using the remaining raffia, tie each cornhusk ring onto the cross twig, two on each side of the post twig. It's fine if extra raffia dangles from the

ties; it will add to the artistry of the wind sock when it blows. Each of the rings should dangle loosely from the crossbar twig.

7. Stake the upright twig in the ground, perhaps in a garden, about a few inches deep. The ends of the husks should not touch the ground. When the wind blows, the little cornhusks of your Natural Wind Sock will twirl, wiggle, and float in the same direction.

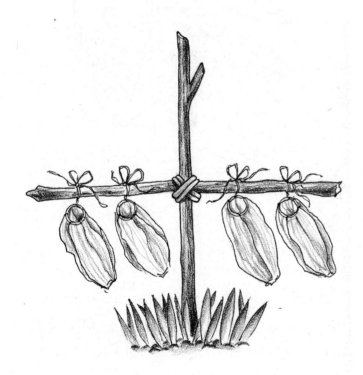

Grass Masks

Ages 6 and under

Ancient people made masks of grasses and clay to celebrate holidays and ceremonies. Many of these ancient masks now hang in museums or decorate the homes of collectors. These Grass Masks are fun to create and make cool costumes to wear when you put on a play or go trick-or-treating. You can also hang your masks on the wall as art.

Materials

Bag for collecting grass
1 paper grocery bag for every mask you want to make
Scissors
Box of colored markers or crayons
Other nature-made items, such as bark or leaves
Decorative items, such as yarn, fabric scraps, or cardboard tubes
Craft glue or homemade Natural Glue, p. xiv

1. Use your collecting bag to gather enough grass to cover one side of a paper grocery bag. Make

sure the grass is dry. If it is not, spread it out in a sunny spot and let it dry for several hours.

2. Cut about 6 inches off the opened end of the grocery bag. The part of the bag that remains will be your mask.

3. Lay the bag flat on your workspace with the closed end away from you.

4. Draw two circles for eyes; also draw a nose and mouth. Cut them out with the scissors.

5. Decorate the face by gluing strips of grass placed in all different directions. Try to cover the entire face. You may also use the bark, leaves, yarn, and other materials.

6. The hair can be added by gluing strips of grass to the top of the bag. Glue one end down to the top of the closed bag. If you use short grass, you will want to glue more, but only one end, about an inch of it, to the bag. The other part of the grass can flow downward or stick out like spiky hair.

7. If you want to pretend that your Grass Mask has a powdered wig or curlers in the hair, you can glue some tissue tubes to the top. You may also want to braid some of the grasses before you glue them to the top for hair.

Cattail Planter

Ages 6 and under

Cattails are a grass that grows on the banks of ponds and streams. In late summer they produce brown fuzzy seedpods that feel soft like the tail of a cat. Put several of these pods together in a Cattail Planter. The rich brown color looks like velvet.

Adult supervision required

Materials

Bag for collecting

15–20 cattails

Scissors

Hairspray

3 sheets old newspaper

Plastic or glass tub or
    pot, 4–5 inches tall

Rubber cement

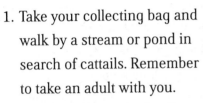

1. Take your collecting bag and walk by a stream or pond in search of cattails. Remember to take an adult with you. (Never go near a body of water by yourself.)

2. Ask the adult to help you snip off 15–20 cattails with your scissors. Tell the adult to cut the cattails just below the fuzzy part. Cattails are a hardy plant that grows in moist areas. Spray lightly with hairspray to keep the seeds from floating off.

3. Cover your table or work area with the sheets of newspaper.

4. Place a strip of rubber cement on your plastic tub running upward and downward on the side.

🍂 Nature Notes

Smart Seeds

A seed is the beginning of life for a plant, flower, and tree. But plants and trees grow everywhere, not just next to the plant where the seeds come from. Seeds go everywhere, so plants and trees can grow in new places and sprout more seeds. How do they do that? Think of a dandelion. When you blow on the white fluffy heads, just as the wind does, those tiny seeds float off to grow in new places. Seeds from maples and sycamore trees have little brown wings that help them fly far away. Another way seeds travel places is by being carried by people, insects, and animals. Think about the seeds in an apple. An apple you buy in a market is far from the tree from which it was picked. Once you finish your apple, you throw away the core and seeds. Wherever they land, a new apple tree can grow!

5. Stick a fuzzy cattail to the pot and hold it in place. Do this until the entire pot or tub is covered with cattails. Let dry. When your Cattail Planter is finished, you can put a plant inside or fill it with water and float flowers or candles in it to make a table centerpiece.

Seed Starter

Ages 6 and under

Another way seeds travel to new places is by sticking to animal fur and human clothing. A simple way to learn about how seeds travel and what types of plants grow from seeds is to make a Seed Starter.

Materials

1 white cotton sock, clean
1 sheet old newspaper
1 string, at least 5 feet long
Clear glass jar
$\frac{1}{2}$ cup of water
Measuring spoon
3 tablespoons vegetable oil
5 drops food coloring
Spoons

1. Crumple one sheet of newspaper and stuff into the cotton sock.
2. Tie the open end of the sock closed using one end of the string.
3. Take your sock on a nature walk through a meadow, field, or forest on a summer day.
4. Pull the sock by the end of the string and let it drag along the ground. When you are done, your sock will be filled with bits of soil, grasses, and plenty of sticky seeds.
5. Bring your sock home. Carry it carefully so that the seeds do not fall off.
6. Mix the vegetable oil, water, and food coloring together. The oil will separate from the water in beads, but the water will turn colors.
7. Pour about an inch of this mixture into your clear glass jar.
8. Stuff your newspaper-filled sock into the jar and watch the water press up along the sides of the glass. After a few days, the seeds stuck to the sock will soon start to sprout up and around the oil and through the colored water.
9. Be sure to keep the sock moist by adding water at least once a week. Put your jar in a sunny spot. You can watch the seeds grow through the glass of your Seed Starter. Try to identify what plants will grow from the different seeds.

Tiny Seed House

Ages 7 and up

This little treasure, covered with the seeds of vegetables and trees, can be used as a dollhouse or hung in a tree to feed birds, squirrels, and other critters. The design is simple to do. You may want to add your own creative talent to make a bigger Tiny Seed House or one that has a chimney.

Materials

30 wooden craft sticks*

Craft glue or homemade Natural Glue, p. xiv

8 pieces twine, each 8 inches long

30 or more small pinecones, about 5 inches in
   length in the shape of a carrot

Scissors

Rubber cement

1 piece thick cardboard, 4 × 8 inches, or throwaway
   metal cookie sheet (an option for use in all types
   of weather)

1 bag soup beans or assorted seeds

*Twigs that lie flat may be used, but you will need to use rubber cement in place of the craft glue.

1. Build your frame. You'll need six craft sticks for each wall and six for the floor. Glue four sticks together to form a square. Glue one running up the middle of your square and one running across the middle.
2. Let all four walls and floor dry well.
3. Build your house. Starting with two walls, stand them so that they meet along the edge. Using the twine, strap the two corners together at the top and the bottom by wrapping the twine around the sticks. You may want to ask someone to hold

the walls while you wrap the twine together. Do this for each wall. Then tie them on the floor.

4. When you are done, you should have a box made from craft sticks (without a top).

5. Put a strip of glue where the edges meet so that your box will hold firmly together. Let this dry.

6. Add the walls. Spreading rubber cement along the outside of the craft sticks, glue as many pinecones as will fit on each wall.

7. Cut one pinecone in half. Put the two halves in the middle so that you will have a door to your house. If you want, you can do this for each side so that the house will have many doors or windows.

8. Continue to glue pinecones until the entire box is covered, including the bottom.

9. Add the roof. Bend the piece of cardboard or metal cookie sheet in half. Then open it up so that it stands in the shape of a triangle.

10. Glue this to the roof of the box by running craft glue along the edges of the sticks. Set the cardboard on top.

11. Using craft glue, cover the entire roof with the beans or seeds and let dry. Your Tiny Seed House is ready to be displayed as art or put outside for wildlife to use.

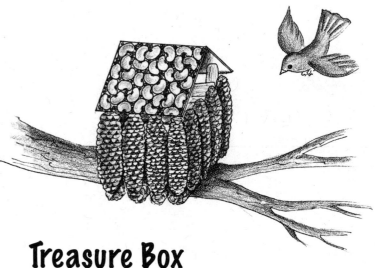

Treasure Box

Ages 6 and under

Have you ever seen seed art or a seed mosaic? A mosaic is a type of art in which small pieces of things, such as tile or glass, are grouped together to form a picture or an interesting design. Mosaic art can be found on the walls and floors of modern buildings. Ancient cultures created mosaics from stones and tiles to decorate buildings and temples. Today many museums, churches, and government buildings still have mosaic-tiled floors. Seeds can also be used to make a mosaic picture. This Treasure Box will use different-colored seeds and beans to decorate a mosaic box of treasures.

Materials

Black marker
Plastic diaper wipes box
Mosaic tile adhesive
1 wooden craft stick
Large bowl filled with dried beans and seeds, different colors

1. With the black marker, draw a design on the top and sides of the diaper wipes box. Trace out the pattern first with pencil. You can draw a picture of a flower, a cat, or anything else you like. You can also draw a pattern instead of an object or animal.

2. Squirt some of the mosaic tile adhesive onto one side of the box in the shape of the pattern or design you created. Spread it out with the craft stick if necessary.

3. Fill in the design with the beans and seeds. Do this by placing them, one by one, onto the mosaic tile adhesive.

4. Continue to glue down the beans and seeds until the whole top is covered. Let dry before moving on to the next side. Be sure to leave the space near the opening uncovered so that the box can be opened and closed easily without disturbing your artwork.

5. When all sides of your box are decorated with seeds, let it dry completely. Your Treasure Box will look very much like the treasure chests found by pirates on the high seas. You can display it as art and store your treasures inside.

Anchors Aweigh

An anchor is something strong that holds an object in place. A boat has an anchor. When it is tossed into the water, the heavy anchor sinks to the bottom and keeps the boat firmly in place. Grasses and plants are anchors, too. They have strong roots that grow into the ground and keep soil and sand in place. People put plants and grass in the ground to protect soil and sand from washing away. Plants and grasses also keep things safe and warm. They hide animals and insects from their enemies. They protect a house against the cold winds. Grassy areas and meadows are where many animals make their home. Insects, small reptiles, and rodents also rely on grassy areas to give them a safe and dry home. When new homes, buildings, or parks are built, grassy areas are cut down or destroyed, causing wildlife, such as the Karner blue butterfly and the prairie dog, to lose their homes. But many organizations are working hard to save grasslands and meadows so that wildlife that live in these grassy places can survive. Some of the organizations hard at work to save grasslands, plants, and wildlife are the Nature Conservancy (www.nature.org), the Buffalo National Grasslands Visitor Center in Wall, South Dakota (www.trailsand grasslands.org/grland.html),

and the United States Forest Service (www.fs.fed.us). They work with volunteers and private organizations to increase the size of existing grasslands and halt building around these protected areas so that wildlife are not harmed or forced to leave. They also harvest seeds to grow more abundant plants in and around grasslands and to stop the spread of harmful species of plants and wildlife that may invade.

You may have already seen some of these organizations at work in your neighborhood. Signs that say *Do Not Mow* are put in places where butterflies are feeding and laying eggs, or snakes are hiding from the hot summer sun. You may also have observed prairie homes being built. Prairie homes are easy to spot because of the plants growing up around them. Prairie home neighborhoods are areas where people do not mow their grass but instead let it grow tall so that wildlife can live and grow there. These neighborhoods are called conservation communities. The families who live there help to protect nature and grow new plants and trees so that wildlife can stay in their habitats for years to come.

5

Animals, Birds, and Insects

Isn't it fun to spot a deer feeding quietly in the woods, or to spy an armadillo across a dusty road? Have you ever tried to catch a cricket or hold a ladybug in your hand and watch it crawl around? All animals, fish, reptiles, birds, and insects are wildlife that rely on the natural resources our earth provides. They need plants to eat and water to drink. They need mountains and trees and soil in which to build homes that will protect them from the heat or cold, and hide them from their enemies. Whether in the ocean, forest, desert, or the green grassy meadows, wildlife creatures need nature in order to survive. The area where they live that provides the things needed to survive is called a *habitat.* (See the Nature Note on habitats on page 94.)

Unfortunately, the natural resources and undeveloped land that once provided food and shelter to animals are beginning to disappear. In some cases wildlife creatures are forced to move into new regions to survive; in other cases they disappear altogether because of the loss of their habitat. Maybe you live in an area where you gradually see more and more deer and wild animals crossing streets and living in backyards and neighborhoods. This type of behavior often happens when animals' homes are destroyed for new construction and they seek shelter elsewhere. Another example is when falcons and eagles can no longer nest high in the mountains, in trees, and on cliffs, and instead are forced to build their homes on top of skyscrapers and bridges.

Look around at all the new buildings, parking lots, schools, landfills, and shopping malls being built. Although the new places we build are important to people, we must be careful about how much of nature we destroy. But there is a brighter side. Many individuals and organizations, such as the World Wildlife Fund (www.worldwildlife.org), are taking steps to help protect wildlife and create safe places where wildlife can live and grow. Many companies are looking at ways to rebuild land that has been cleared for construction, or to turn old abandoned buildings into something new and exciting, such as creative living spaces or offices. Many communities are encouraging builders to restore old buildings instead of clearing land to build new ones.

Communities are developing parks, nature trails, and other green spaces so that everyone can learn to appreciate our natural world.

You don't have to be an adult to help save wildlife. There are many ways you can protect wildlife, provide new sources of food and shelter, and teach others to respect animals, fish, birds, insects, and all living organisms. This chapter contains great ideas for helping wildlife. It also shows you how to make beautiful, earth-friendly art that will remind everyone that wildlife is an important part of our earth family.

Here are two wonderful books to learn more about protecting wildlife:

For Kids Who Love Animals: A Guide to Sharing the Planet by Linda Koebner. New York: Berkley Books, 1993. (Ages 4–8)
World Wildlife Fund by Jillian Powell. New York: Franklin Watts, 2001. (Ages 7–10)

Wildlife Seedling Tray

Ages 6 and under

A great way to watch animals, birds, and insects up close is to grow a wildlife garden. A wildlife garden is a special garden because it contains plants and trees that provide food and shelter for wildlife. A Wildlife Seedling Tray is the first place to start growing the plants and trees that will provide new homes and sources of food for animals, birds, and insects. You may also want to give a Wildlife Seedling Tray to someone as a gift. By doing so, you'll help to teach others that wildlife is an important part of our earth.

Materials

Cardboard egg carton
1 sheet plastic wrap, 16–20 inches long
Pen
Box of colorful markers
Gardening gloves
Spoon
Potting soil
12 packages assorted seeds
Scissors
Roll of clear tape
12 wooden craft sticks
1 cup water

1. Remove the lid from your egg carton by tearing or cutting it off. Or ask an adult to help you.
2. Cover the entire lid of your egg carton with the plastic wrap. This will be the tray for under your egg carton cups.
3. Use the pen point to gently poke one or two small holes in the bottom of each cup.
4. Use markers to decorate the sides of the egg carton. Be sure to color each cup on the outside. Use any design you choose.
5. Now turn the bottom portion of your decorated egg carton right side up.
6. Put on your gardening gloves. Add two spoonfuls of potting soil to each cup with your spoon.
7. Add your seeds. Carefully open each seed packet and put three or four seeds in each cup. Each cup should contain a different type of seed. Make sure to put the seed packet next to the cup so that you know what type of seed is in each cup.

🦫 Nature Notes

Habitats

One of the best ways to enjoy nature is by taking a walk in the woods or a meadow, and seeing animals, birds, and insects in their natural habitats. A *habitat* is a place in the environment where a creature naturally lives or grows. For example, the habitat of a polar bear is a very cold place with water nearby, such as in Alaska. The habitat for a crocodile is a warm, shady, water-filled area, such as the Florida Everglades. If you look out your window, you'll see the habitat of many animals in your neighborhood. Thick shrubs and bushes provide a natural habitat for rabbits to burrow underneath. Oak trees provide food and shelter for many types of squirrels.

8. Put two more spoonfuls of potting soil on top of each seed.

9. Gently press the potting soil down in each cup.

10. Carefully fold the top of the seed packets over so that they're sealed and no seeds will spill out. Secure with tape.

11. Tape each packet of seeds to the top of a craft stick, making sure the name of the plant seed can still be seen. It should look like a seed packet lollipop!

12. Take each seed packet lollipop and put it in the dirt near the end of each cup that contains its seeds. Fasten in place with tape. This will help you remember what type of plant is in each cup. You'll also have more seeds handy to grow another Wildlife Seedling Tray once you have planted yours in a garden outside.

13. Put your Wildlife Seedling Tray on top of the plastic-covered egg carton top. This tray will catch any water that drains from your seedling cups.

14. Finally, add a little bit of water to each cup, making sure that it does not overflow. You won't over water if you dip your finger in the water and let 5 to 10 droplets fall into each cup. You are now ready to put your Wildlife Seedling Tray in a sunny spot where it can grow. Be sure to add a

little water each week. When your seedlings begin to sprout and grow several inches high, they are ready to plant outside. Remember to add other things to your garden to make it a great place for wildlife to live. Rocks and a low-lying water dish will provide shelter and a water source for lizards, toads, and turtles. In addition, letting the grass grow tall in a patch of your garden will provide shelter and food for rabbits, chipmunks, butterflies, and dragonflies. Watch how birds, insects, and animals eat from or use your plants to make a new home.

Your Wildlife Garden

The best way to choose plants to grow in your wildlife garden is to think about the types of things wildlife needs to survive. Birds eat berries and seeds, so choose plants like sunflowers or winterberries to grow in your garden. Amphibians and water-loving creatures need moist places to live, so choose plants like ferns or hostas that need a lot of moisture, and provide shady areas for toads and turtles to hide. Here's a guide to help you get started with planting your wildlife garden.

Some plants will not grow in every climate, so ask an adult to help you to pick the best plants for the region where you live. Remember that these are only a few examples of plants that attract wildlife. A great way to learn about plants to grow, wildlife diets, and habitats where you live is to contact your local gardening club, which is often registered with your local library. (Or go to http://garden web.com to find a listing of gardening clubs.)

To Attract	Plant
Baltimore oriole	Apple trees
Blue jay	Oak trees, sunflowers, cornstalks
Butterflies	Grass and butterfly bush
Cardinals	Sunflowers
Dragonflies	Tall grasses, such as cattails and ribbon grass
Evening Grosbeak	Pine trees
Hummingbird	Heliconia flowers, lupine bluebonnets, and snapdragons
Goldfinch	Thistle
Ladybugs	Fennel, dill, tansy, and yarrow
Woodpeckers	Saguaro cacti, oak trees

Toad Home

Ages 7 and up

Toads are amphibians—smooth-skinned animals that are born in water and transform in shape and size as they grow into adults. They're in between fish and reptiles. A tadpole is an amphibian. When it grows to an adult it becomes a frog or a toad. Although they like living near water, toads actually prefer to be on land. They like moist and shady places, such as gardens, where they can stay cool and hidden away from enemies. They are often found hopping around at night on a summer's evening, looking for worms, beetles, and crickets to eat. This Toad Home will give them shady shelter on a sunny day.

Adult supervision required

Materials

Thick rubber-palmed gardening gloves or
    construction gloves
Lab safety glasses or work goggles
Old or unwanted terracotta flowerpot with a
    drainage hole in the bottom
Old bath towel
Wooden-handled hammer
Old piece pottery or china that has been broken or
    discarded
3 sheets old newspaper
20 small stones or pebbles, assorted colors
Mosaic tile adhesive
Potting soil
1 rock, size of your palm

1. Ask an adult to assist you. Put on the gloves and the safety glasses to protect your hands and eyes. The adult should do so, too.
2. With the bottom opening of the terracotta pot facing up, cover it with the old bath towel.
3. Holding the towel-covered pot with one hand, ask an adult to use the hammer to gently tap away at one section of the rim of the pot. Continue tapping until a U-shaped hole about the size of your fist has been removed from the rim of the pot.
4. Uncover the pot. Hold the head of the hammer and lay the handle flat on top of the rim of the pot. Run it slowly around the rim, back and forth a few times, to smooth out any rough edges. You

may also need to move the handle like a saw, moving it forward and back, over any rough edges within the entryway you've created.

5. Put the three sheets of newspaper on a sidewalk, patio, or workbench.

6. Put the old pottery or china on top of the newspaper.

7. Cover the pottery with the bath towel.

8. Using your hammer or letting an adult do it, gently break up the pottery into 1-inch pieces.

9. Now it's time to decorate your terracotta pot. Using the mosaic tile adhesive, stick pieces of your broken pottery, stones, and pebbles all over the outside of your pot. Take care not to cover the hole on the bottom. Be sure to wear your gloves so that you're not cut by the broken pottery.

10. Let the terracotta pot dry well in the sun.

11. Find a place to set up your Toad Home that's cool and shady, where it will not be disturbed. A corner of a garden or an edge of a patio is good. Place a handful of potting soil in the center of the spot where you plan to build your Toad Home. This potting soil will be covered by the pot, but will provide a soft, moist place for the toad to sit and sleep or wait for food. Now turn the pot upside down over the handful of potting soil.

12. Loosely place more potting soil around the outside of the pot, but make sure to leave the U-shaped doorway open. Build the potting soil up around the pot so that about 2 inches of the outside of the pot is covered. Place a rock on top of the pot to cover the hole in what used to be the bottom of the pot. The weight of the decorative stones and china will help to hold your Toad Home firmly in place during summer rainstorms. On a summer's night, remove the rock on top to peek inside. With the help of a flashlight you can see how many toads have made this cool, shady hideaway their home.

Porcupine

Ages 6 and under

Another way that animals protect themselves in nature is to have a defense system. Skunks use a smelly spray as a defense against enemies. Cheetahs run fast and far. Porcupines wiggle and poke potential predators with their long, prickly quills. This artistic Porcupine has prickly quills, too!

Materials

1 cup air-dry modeling clay or Homemade Salt Clay*
1 small plastic juice jug
2 wiggle eyes or 2 buttons
1 rock that will cover opening of juice bottle
4 twigs, each 1 inch long
Bag pine needles

1. Cover the plastic juice jug with modeling clay. Smooth it out all over.
2. Stick two wiggle eyes or buttons above the bottle opening and use the rock to close the opening. The rock should be larger than the opening and should stick when pressed into the modeling clay.
3. The Porcupine needs some legs. Poke the four twigs into the modeling clay on the underside of the juice bottle, two in front and two in back. (It's up to you to decide which side of the bottle will be the underside and which the top.)
4. Gently cover the entire back of the Porcupine with the pine needles.
5. If you are using dried pine needles, be very gentle. They break more easily than fresh ones. Fresh pine needles often fall off trees when seasons change or when wind, animals, or birds knock them away. After pine needles fall to the ground, they will be used by animals for nests. They decompose and are absorbed by the soil to help make it healthy for new plants to grow. We can also use pine needles for crafts, but remember to only use pine needles that you find on the ground. Pulling living leaves and needles from a tree can damage it.
6. Put the Porcupine in a sunny spot to dry, but be careful. Just like a real one, this Porcupine has very prickly quills!

2. Slowly add all of the water and vegetable oil to the flour-and-salt mixture. Stir until it comes together in a lump.

3. Using your hands, roll and slide the lump between your palms to form a smooth ball.

4. Your Homemade Salt Clay is ready to use and shape. When you finish shaping the clay, let it dry well in a warm and sunny spot for at least one day.

5. Homemade Salt Clay can also be baked in an oven at 250° F (121° C) for 1 hour if it is used only to make shapes. But do *not* bake it when combined with plastic, twigs, stones, or any other ingredient. Remember, never use an oven or stove alone. Always ask an adult for help.

Textured Turkey

Ages 6 and under

Turkeys are a breed of bird with all types of crazy colors and textures. Baby turkeys, called *poults*, have a soft and fluffy feel from their soft *downy* feathers, or baby feathers. When these fall off, colorful new ones grow in their place. These feathers can be yellow,

*Homemade Salt Clay Recipe

Measuring cups

2 cups flour

1 cup salt

Mixing bowl

Spoon

1 cup water

1½ tablespoons vegetable oil

Measuring spoons

1. Pour flour and salt into the mixing bowl. Mix well with a spoon.

Nature Notes

Feather Facts

Did you know that the average bird has from 1,000 to 4,000 feathers? In general, the larger the bird, the more feathers it has. Some larger birds, such as the turkey, have only 3,000 feathers. The duck, a smaller bird, has as many as 13,000 feathers. Each bird's feathers form a unique pattern, making the bird easy to identify and beautiful to look at. Male and female birds have different feather patterns and colors. The male birds are more colorful. But feathers also are used for protection. The millions of colors found in feathers *camouflage* (CAM-oo-flazh), or hide, a bird from its enemies. Female birds often have plain, earth-colored feathers so that they blend in well with trees or the ground as they sit on their eggs or as they protect and feed their young. Amazingly, the feathers of some birds change throughout the year. A goldfinch grows new feathers that blend in with the plants that grow during different seasons. The colors of birds' feathers come from their parents, just like our hair and eye color. The colored feathers help the birds to blend in with their environment. Feathers also protect a bird's skin, keep it warm and dry, gain the attention of other birds, and help it to fly. Birds shed their feathers during a process called *molting*, which occurs up to three times a year. Most birds molt in the spring and again at the end of the summer during nesting season. At this time birds that fly stay close to the ground while their new flying feathers grow. Feathers may be found everywhere during molting, but the feathers of many birds, such as those of songbirds, hawks, owls, and eagles, should never be picked up or taken from the spot where they were found. Instead let them be, because certain birds and their feathers are protected by the United States Fish and Wildlife Services. Check out www.fws.gov/educators/students.html for more information about birds and their protection.

brown, green, blue, black, or snowy white. Turkeys come in all colors and shapes. Some are thinner and have long tail feathers. Some are round and too fat to fly. But all turkeys have one thing in common: feathers don't grow on their heads. Instead they have bumpy, hairy skin, sometimes colored red and sometimes blue. They also have a piece of skin, called a *wattle*, which hangs from the throat and wiggles when they gobble.

This craft is called Textured Turkey because it isn't just something to look at but something for you to feel. When you are all done with your turkey, gently rub your hands over the art and you'll feel the soft, prickly textures of nature.

Materials

Scissors

2 pieces construction paper, $8\frac{1}{2} \times 11$ inches, one brown or tan, one red, gold, yellow, or orange

Pencil

Scissors

3 pinecones, dry

Old washcloth, damp

Gardening gloves

Tacky glue

20–30 leaves shaped like feathers, blades of dried
    grass or thin twigs, at least 4 inches in length

1 small piece red construction paper, 1 × 1 inch

1 ¼-inch wiggle eye or small button

1. Trace your hand with a pencil on the sheet of
   darker construction paper.

2. Using your scissors, carefully cut out your hand
   pattern. This hand pattern is the base of your
   turkey.

3. Carefully pull as many scales off your pinecones
   as you can and set them in a pile. The scales of a
   pinecone are the petal parts that make up the
   whole seed or cone. An easy way to remove the
   scales from a pinecone is to first soak the
   pinecone in water for 2–3 hours. Next, cover the
   pinecone with a washcloth and gently roll it
   back and forth between your hands to loosen
   the scales. Some pinecones have prickly scales,
   so you may want to put on a pair of gardening
   gloves before you begin.

4. Take the second sheet of construction paper and
   shred it into tiny pieces about the same size as
   your pinecone scales. Put them in a pile next to
   your pinecone scales.

5. Along the fingers of your hand pattern, glue
   down your leaves, grass, or twigs with the tacky
   glue to make pretend feathers.

6. You can overlap the leaves, grass, or twigs if you
   want to give the turkey thick tail feathers.

7. Using your scissors, cut a teardrop shape from
   your piece of red construction paper.

8. Glue the tip of the teardrop on to the tip of the
   thumb of your hand pattern. Make sure that the
   big base of the teardrop is hanging down. This
   will be the turkey's wattle, the little red fleshy
   piece that hangs from a turkey's beak.

9. Spread a layer of glue all over the remaining
   portion of your hand pattern from the tip of your
   thumb to the tip of the pretend feathers.

10. Stick a mixture of pinecone scales and shredded construction paper all over. Cover the entire turkey body.

11. Put a drop of tacky glue on the back of the wiggle eye or button. Glue the eye onto the middle of the thumb part of your hand pattern. Now your Textured Turkey is complete. Make sure to let it dry well before you hang it up. Everyone will enjoy looking at and touching the texture of your turkey.

Gourd Birdhouse

Ages 7 and up

For many years gourds have been used as pottery, bird houses, and decorations. The shell of a gourd is hard, and when dried from the inside out can be a very useful tool. Birds like gourds because they are warm inside and the small holes keep away unwanted intruders. Watch for the cave dweller birds and birds that like dark, quiet places. They are the ones that would want to make your birdhouse their home. The birds that like dark, quiet places include wrens, sparrows, starlings, nuthatches, chickadees, purple martins, and woodpeckers.

The best time to build the Gourd Birdhouse is in the spring. This is the time when small birds look for places to nest in and build a home for their young.

Adult supervision required

Materials

Thick rubber-palmed gardening gloves or construction gloves

3 sheets old newspaper

1 medium-sized hard-shell gourd, such as a bottle, lady, kettle, or basket gourd (These gourds have big bottoms and smaller tops and are shaped like peanuts.)

2–3 metal cookie cutters in various shapes, including a round one

Power drill

Large metal spoon

1 piece nylon cord, 10 inches

1. Put on your gloves to protect your hands.
2. Spread the newspapers down to protect your workspace.

3. Using the round cookie cutter, press a circle shape in the center of the gourd.

4. Ask an adult to drill a hole in the gourd using the circle shape as a pattern with the drill. You might want to help by using a marker to indicate the spot.

5. Now have the adult drill a small hole through the neck of the gourd and two or three smaller holes in the bottom of the gourd for drainage.

6. Insert the metal spoon in the hole in the center of the gourd and pull out the pulp and seeds.

7. Weave the nylon cord through the neck of the gourd. Tie it securely in a knot on top. This will be used to hang your gourd from a tree or hook.

8. Use the remaining cookie cutters to lightly press shapes into the exterior of the gourd for decoration.

9. Place your gourd on newspapers. Let it dry in the sun for at least 24 hours, or in a cool, dry place throughout the winter season. When the gourd dries, the cookie cutter shapes will turn brown, giving the Gourd Birdhouse a pretty pattern.

10. Hang up your Gourd Birdhouse in a quiet spot where you can watch the action without disturbing the birds.

Birdbath

Ages 6 and under

This is an easy craft that uses just about anything and everything you find in the wild. Birds love to drink and splash in small water sources. Put a birdbath in your garden or on your doorstep. As you watch the fun, you will learn more about the types of birds that live in your neighborhood. You may also want to keep a camera handy. Some of the best nature pictures are of birds splashing in a backyard Birdbath!

Materials

Bag for collecting all types of small things found in nature, such as twigs, stones, leaves, grasses, nuts, or bark

3 rocks, size of your fist

1 throwaway pie pan

Craft glue or homemade Natural Glue, p. xiv

Water source

1. Go on a nature walk and collect all types of small things to decorate your birdbath. Items such as twigs, stones, leaves, grasses, nuts, and bark will work nicely.
2. Place your three rocks on the table or workspace. Set your pie pan on top upside down. Move your pie pan so that it is tilted, with one side resting on the rocks and the other on the table. The first side you'll be working with is the one tilted upward.
3. Squirt some glue on the outside edge of the pan and stick your nature collection to it. Fasten the things you found on your nature walk to the *rim* of the pan, not the bottom.
4. Twigs, leaves—whatever you like. Just cover the outside edge of your pan completely with natural things.
5. When the glue dries, you are ready to put your Birdbath outside.
6. Place the three large rocks inside the pan before you add the water. The rocks will hold your pan in place on windy days and give birds something to perch on.
7. Fill your pan with water. Be sure it to refill it regularly to keep the water fresh and clean. Now watch the birds appear in your Birdbath.

Dandelion Chicks

Ages 7 and up

Some people think of the dandelion plant as a weed. Others understand that the leaves are nutritious and make great salads. One thing we all know is that dandelions are everywhere. Because of their strong roots and bright colors, they are often unwanted in the lawn. Instead of spraying them with poisons, save the environment and turn these weeds into nature-made animals, such as Dandelion Chicks.

Materials

2 small pieces orange construction paper

Scissors

Craft glue or homemade Natural Glue, p. xiv

2 Styrofoam eggs or two sheets old newspaper crumpled into 2 balls

30 or more yellow dandelion heads

4 wiggle eyes or small black buttons

1 small basket or bowl

Bunch of green or dried grasses

1. Cut out two triangle-shaped pieces from the construction paper for the chick's beak. Fold the flat part of the triangle over one fold. Glue this flat piece to the end of each Styrofoam egg or newspaper ball. Hold in place until it dries.

2. Using the glue, cover the eggs with dandelion heads and let dry.

3. Glue two wiggle eyes or buttons above the beaks.

Nature Notes

Bird Watcher

Now that you have built your very own birdhouse and birdbath, you can become a bird watcher. Pick a spot where you can sit and watch your birdhouse or birdbath. Be very quiet so that you do not scare the birds away. A pair of binoculars will help you to see the birds more closely. This activity will make a great science project, so don't forget to get out your nature journal and write down what you observe. The following questions will help you learn about the bird family living in your birdhouse.

- What do the birds look like (color, size, shape)?
- What type of nesting materials and food do the birds take into the birdhouse?
- Are there baby birds in the house? Do you know when they were hatched?
- Do the birds change how often they leave the house during different seasons?

Finding answers to these questions will help you to identify the type of birds that live in your house.

4. Fill the bowl with the green or dried grasses. Set your two chicks inside.

If you'd like to save your Dandelion Chicks, or any flowers you may collect, you can dry the flower heads. You'll need a large plastic container with a lid, rubber gloves, and a package of silica gel (available at a craft store or you can collect small packets of silica gel that come with store-bought products, such as leather shoes and purses). Put on your rubber gloves. If you are using small packets of silica gel, be sure that you have 2 cups. Place 1 cup of the silica gel crystals in the plastic container. Carefully place the dandelion heads on top of the gel. Cover them with the remaining silica gel and close the container tightly.

Let the container sit for 2 weeks. By then your dandelion heads will be permanently dried, and your Dandelion Chicks will last a long time. Another way to dry flowers is to hang them upside down in your closet, basement, or garage. Leave them hanging for at least a week. Experiment with different types of flowers, and try different art and crafts projects with them. Many flowers wilt when dried, and their colors become dull. Some flowers, such as strawflowers and purple statice, remain bright and colorful.

Caterpillar Critter

Ages 6 and under

This is a great craft to make in the fall, when many flowers are dying or drying. Using the flowers at the end of their blooming cycle will extend the time you can enjoy their beauty. This cool critter will get many second looks. Just when you think it's a growing garden, take a closer look and you'll find a soft little Caterpillar Critter resting in the grass.

Materials

3 sheets old newspaper
Package plastic wrap

1 ready-made plastic picture frame, clear acrylic
    box frame with the cardboard insert removed, or
    old picture frame with glass or plastic still inside,
    or even old serving tray. (Any picture frame or
    tray that has a flat bottom and sides at least
    1 inch high will work for this project.)

Potting soil

Spoon

Grass seed

Water

4 florist's foam balls or crumpled-up newspaper
    balls, 2–3 inches in size.

3 bunches dried yarrow or any yellow-colored
    flower that will dry, such as strawflowers

Scissors

Craft glue or homemade Natural Glue, p. xiv

30 or more black-eyed Susans, asters, or any other
    flowers with dark-colored centers

2 small twigs, each 2 inches long

2 wiggle eyes or small white buttons

1. Spread several sheets of newspaper on the table
    or workspace.

2. Cover the entire picture frame or serving tray
    with clear plastic wrap. Be sure to wrap it com-
    pletely, including the back, so that none of the
    soil or water will leak.

🦅 *Nature Notes*

It's a Small World

There are more than 1 million different known *species* of insects. A *species* is a group of living creatures of the same kind that can breed together. Some experts estimate that there may be as many as 10 million—most yet to be discovered! Some insects are so small that we can barely see them with our eyes. Some insects are fun to pick up and look at, like a ladybug with spotted wings, or a firefly that glows in the dark. Other insects are dangerous and should not be touched. Tarantulas, wasps, and fire ants can be poisonous and harmful to humans and animals. But even these insects are important to our world. They are part of the *food chain*, the link of food that starts with very small plants and organisms and works its way up to humans. If these insects were to disappear, so would the creatures that eat them for food. This would set our natural world and ecosystem off balance. Big or small, friendly or dangerous, all the insects that make up this small world are important to us.

Entomologists (ent-o-MALL-o-gists) are people who study insects. These scientists have a very important job. They study insects and discover new ones. They teach us about where insects live, what they eat, what things they do, and whether they are friendly to us. Entomologists also write books and create museum exhibits so that we can learn all about this very small world.

See this Web page for more insect fun: www.earthlife.net/insects.

Honeycombs

Honeybees are a type of insect that lives in hives. Hives are big colonies where bees live and work, make honey, and build a home for new bees to be born. Worker bees build the new home, or honeycomb, where the queen honeybee lays her eggs. Worker bees produce a waxy substance that allows them to create hundreds of six-sided cells. When put together, these cells make a giant honeycomb. New bees are born in the honeycomb. Nectar from flowers is turned into honey and stored in the honeycomb. Honey made in honeycombs is sweet to taste and smell.

3. Inside the frame or tray, spoon out a thin layer of potting soil.

4. Spread grass seed all over the top of the soil. Water lightly by dipping your fingers into a cup of water and then letting the water drip down over the soil. You should do this dipping and dripping about three times a week. If the soil is very dry, then dip and drip everyday until it becomes moist. It will take several weeks for your grassy ground to grow, so keep your frame in a sunny spot and lightly watered.

5. Now make your little caterpillar. Cover two of the foam balls with the heads of the dried yarrow or other dried gold flower. The tops of these flowers should just poke into the foam balls, but you may need to add a little glue to the stems to secure them. If you live in an area where yarrow doesn't grow, then you can use other things, such as golden leaves or yellow goldenrod.

6. The other two foam balls should be dark-colored. Cover them with the spongy centers of black-eyed Susans or dark leaves.

7. When the balls are covered, let them dry.

8. Stick the two twigs in the top of one of the balls for antennae. Glue the two wiggle eyes or buttons on the front of the ball.

9. Put your four covered foam balls in the center of the frame. Be sure to put the head in the front. Soon your Caterpillar Critter will be surrounded by a cocoon of grass.

Honey Hive

Ages 6 and under

If you have ever seen a beehive, you know that it usually looks like a giant dome made of a papery substance. Inside there are hundreds of golden combs, each with six sides, and the rich smell of pure honey. This Honey Hive celebrates all the hard work the honeybee does by looking and smelling like the outside and inside of a beehive.

Materials

1 empty Yoplait yogurt container, washed and cleaned, or any other container that is shaped like a triangle and has an opening smaller than the wider bottom

Craft glue or homemade Natural Glue, p. xiv

1 spool of twine

Scissors

Clothespin

3–4 honeycomb-shaped pieces of cereal

1 small piece yellow-colored plastic wrap

1/4 cup of water

Small bunch of honeysuckle flowers

1. Squirt some glue around the outside of the yogurt container.
2. Holding the end of the twine with your finger at the bottom of the container, wrap the twine around the outside of the container until it is completely covered. Wrap the twine carefully, one row on top of the next, so that you cannot see the plastic container underneath.
3. Snip the end of the twine at the top. Secure it with a clothespin for about an hour or until it dries completely.
4. You may need to squirt some more glue onto the twine so that it will hold firmly when dry. Let the twine dry completely before continuing.
5. When completely dry, glue the honeycombs on top of the twine around the container anywhere you like.
6. Taking the plastic wrap, tear off two or three pieces at least 4 inches long. Roll each piece between your fingers or on your worktable until it becomes a crinkly little strip, much like a rolled-up piece of twine.
7. Glue the strips on top of the twine so that they hang from the opening in the top. This will look like golden honey dripping from your hive.
8. Carefully fill your hive halfway with water. Inside it put a bunch of honeysuckle flowers or any other flowers that are available. Set your Honey Hive outdoors. It will attract people as well as bees!

Caution: Bees are fun to watch and learn from, but if they feel threatened by something or someone, they may sting. If you see a bee visit your honeycomb or a garden of flowers, stay away and stand very still. Bees are busy at work collecting pollen and should never be touched. Instead watch from a window, from a distance, or with an adult to guide you.

Mosshopper

Ages 7 and up

Late in the summer, when you run through the tall grass, little green grasshoppers pop up everywhere. In some areas where the weather is warmer and dry, you may see many buzzing locusts flying by. A *locust* is a type of grasshopper. Grasshoppers can jump and sing. They make music by rubbing their legs against their wings. This little grasshopper is green like the grass, but instead of wings he has moss on his back. You can learn more about grasshoppers and locusts at www.kidcyber.com.au/topics/grasshops.htm.

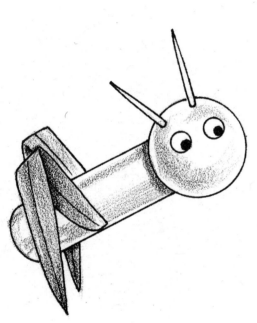

Materials

3 sheets old newspaper

Craft glue or homemade Natural Glue, p. xiv

Toilet tissue tube

Large chunks of moss, about 4 inches long. (Moss can be found on forest floors or in moist grassy areas. If you live in a region where there's no moss, such as the desert Southwest, you can use green paper instead.)

Styrofoam or newspaper ball, 2–3 inches in size.

5 × 7 inch piece green tissue or construction paper

Scissors

2 wiggle eyes or small buttons

2 toothpicks

2 pieces wide green grass, 8 inches long

1. Spread your newspaper on your workspace or table.
2. Put some glue on the paper tube. Gently cover the tube completely with the green moss. Set aside to dry.
3. Put glue on the Styrofoam or newspaper ball. Cover it with the green tissue.
4. Glue on the two wiggle eyes or buttons.
5. Stick the two toothpicks above the eyes. Your Mosshopper's head is now complete with eyes and antennae.
6. Put plenty of glue around one end of the moss-covered tube. Stick your Mosshopper's head to its body.
7. Hold firmly until it begins to dry. Then, set it on the paper. Let it dry completely.
8. Bend each grass blade in half and glue on the sides of the moss-covered tube. The leg should be in the shape of a triangle. Let everything dry completely. Then, show off your Mosshopper art from the earth.

Winter Garland

Ages 7 and up

During the cold months of the year, many animals, birds, and insects *hibernate*, or go underground or inside caves to sleep away the cold months. Others fly to warmer climates in search of comfortable temperatures. Some animals, such as the moose, cardinal, and arctic fox, stay in one area throughout the year, even when temperatures turn colder. Nature provides for these animals by giving them thicker coats and food such as wild berries, evergreens, and bark. You can help feed creatures, too, by making a Winter Garland that decorates your home and provides food for winter wildlife. This is a fun craft to make on a cold winter's day with your friends and family.

Materials

Large sewing needle
1 spool string or thin yarn
Mixing bowl
1 cup birdseed
1 cup crushed nuts
1 cup oatmeal
Spoon
1 cup peanut butter
1 bag mini-bagels
1 bowl popped popcorn
1 bowl dried fruit, such as raisins,
    oranges, apricots
Camera

1. Thread your needle with a very long piece of string or yarn. Tie a big knot at one end and set aside.
2. Pour the birdseed, crushed nuts, and oatmeal into the bowl. Mix with the spoon.
3. Using the spoon, spread a thin layer of peanut butter on all of the bagels.
4. Dip the peanut butter–covered bagels in the mixture of nuts and seed and set aside. You are now ready to string your Winter Garland.
5. Push your threaded needle through several pieces of popcorn, some dried fruit, and the seeded mini-bagels. Continue to do this until you have a long garland of food. If you are working as a group, you can each make shorter garlands and tie them together.

6. When complete, hang your Winter Garland on a tree outside. Keep the camera nearby. You will snap the best wildlife pictures ever as creatures come to feast on your welcome winter treat.

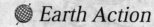 *Earth Action*

Animal Rescue

Sometimes animals are hurt in the wild. A bird with a broken wing may be unable to fly. A raccoon could be stuck in a trap. A baby squirrel may lose its mother. Sometimes hurt or injured animals can be dangerous because they are scared and may try to bite. Never try to touch an animal in the wild, especially if it's hurt. You can help it by contacting an animal rescuer. The Humane Society of the United States is a great place to start. This Web page will help you find your local Humane Society office where you can call to find a rescuer in your area: www.hsus.org. You can also try Wildlife International at www.wildlife-international.org for a listing of rehabilitators and rescuers nationwide. Click the "Emergency" link for information. Check out these great sites to locate a rescuer near you. Keep their number by your phone, or inside your earth art kit, so you can call them quickly if you encounter an injured animal in the wild. You can also write to Orphaned and Injured Wildlife, Inc., Rural Route Box 5650, Spirit Lake, IA 51360 for more information about protecting wildlife and how you can help.

6
Reduce, Reuse, and Recycle

This chapter includes activities that are very important to help protect our earth. You will not only find more craft ideas here, but you'll learn how you can help protect the environment. *Reduce* means to use less of something. When you use less, you are wasting less. Instead of ordering a super-large container of french fries, order only what you can eat. By doing so you will have reduced the amount of food you might waste. Reduce also means to use less packaging. For example, you may choose to take a reusable basket or cloth bag of your own to the grocery store instead of always bringing groceries home in plastic bags they give you. Another way to reduce is to support busi-

nesses and people who use less packaging. Very often when we buy something it comes in elaborately wrapped package with way too much plastic, cardboard, tissue, and paper. A lot of chemicals and resources are needed to create all this packaging and most of it is thrown away. If everyone cut back and asked businesses to also cut back, our amount of waste could be greatly reduced.

Reuse means to find another use for something, use something more than once, or repair broken items so they can be used again. A bicycle you have outgrown can be donated to a charity to be used by someone else. Many of the crafts in this book find new uses for items you might otherwise throw away (or, maybe, recycle), such as the cardboard at the end of a used toilet-paper roll. What was once about to be garbage is now art! *Recycle* means turning waste into something new. In "Soil, Clay, and Sand" (chapter 3), we learned how to compost and make homemade soil. This is a form of recycling: turning wasted food and lawn clippings into something new—soil—that helps new things grow that feed us!

Why are reducing, reusing, and recycling so important? These three actions help cut back on the amount of waste we produce. Imagine if the garbage truck stopped at your door and wanted to dump all the trash in your backyard or neighborhood. You would say no way. No one wants waste dumped in his or her backyard. Littering our environment with plastics, metals, chemicals, and other manufactured materials is not a healthy way to live. But there are only a few places where waste can be safely dumped. The good news is that governments, public organizations, and neighborhoods in many places are starting or expanding recycling programs. Reducing, reusing, and recycling are three ways you can help to turn trash around. The crafts in this book embrace all three of these principles. You'll find more ideas in the "Resources" section in the back of this book, at your local library, or on the Internet.

Clip-and-Snip Cards

Ages 6 and under

Every year around the holidays, thousands of cards are sent to family and friends. Most of these cards are just thrown away after the holidays. You can reduce the amount of paper waste by calling someone on the phone or sending an electronic card via e-mail. When you receive cards, don't just make more trash. Instead get out your scissors and make Clip-and-Snip Cards.

Materials

Old holiday and birthday cards

Old magazines and newspapers

Scissors

8½ × 11–inch pieces of paper (paper that has printing on one side is fine)

Craft glue or homemade Natural Glue, p. xiv

Markers, crayons, or pens

Items found in nature such as grasses, flowers, leaves

Mod Podge, gloss finish

Cup

Paintbrush, 1 inch wide

1. Cut out pictures from old cards, magazines, and newspapers. Lay them out to form a new work of art, design, or picture. Perhaps you will make a bouquet of flowers from all the flower pictures you cut out.

2. Cut the scrap paper in half. Fold each half one time down the middle to make a blank card.

3. Glue the cut-out pictures on the top.

4. Decorate with grasses, flowers, and leaves. Use markers, crayons, and pens, too. Let dry.

5. Put a little Mod Podge in the cup. With your paintbrush, cover your artwork with a glossy coat. This will help keep all the parts in place and make your Clip-and-Snip Cards shine.

Winter Scene Art

Ages 6 and under

Isn't it great when a package is delivered to your home? If it's something breakable that needed protection while shipping, then there's also Styrofoam peanuts and plastic bubble wrap. But what happens to all of that packing material when you are through? Styrofoam peanuts are not easily recycled and

Nature Notes

Just Say No!

By just saying no we can reduce the amount of waste we produce. When you go to the store to buy a new toy, just say no thanks when they offer you a bag. By taking fewer plastic or paper bags home, you are reducing waste. And if you do take a bag home, you can either recycle it or find a new use for it in your home. Remember, if you take a cloth bag to the store to carry your packages home, you are reducing (no plastic bag), reusing, and recycling (the cloth bag won't create any additional waste).

Do you buy new clothes for school each fall? Maybe this year you can wear some of your older clothes that still fit and are still in fashion. This will help our environment in many ways. First, you are not throwing them away and filling up our garbage dumps. Also, when we buy less, we encourage businesses to produce less and cut back on using resources. Think about exchanging clothes with friends and family. Make a party where everyone can bring a bag of clothes, hats, coats, and accessories to trade with everyone else! Any clothing that doesn't make the trade can be donated to charity!

When you are offered a paper napkin, just say no and use a cloth one instead. You can create napkin rings for everyone in your family. Decorate each ring uniquely. Put the names of your family members on their rings. That way each person will have his or her own personal napkin ring. When the cloth napkin gets dirty, you can wash it and use it again and again, instead of throwing it in the garbage like a paper napkin.

Ask your parents to call companies that send catalogs and advertising that fill up your mailbox and just say no, you don't want any more junk mail. Buying fewer new toys, picking products with less cardboard and plastic packaging, exchanging clothes rather than buying new ones, using cloth napkins, taking shorter showers, and using less water all help to reduce waste. Can you think of other ways to just say no?

usually end up in the trash. As we just learned, it is best to reduce the amount of packaging by refusing it. But you cannot always do so. In that case, store the packaging from boxes for reuse. Or you can bag your Styrofoam and deliver it to a mail and package-shipping store for them to reuse. Another way to reuse Styrofoam is to turn it into Winter Scene Art.

Materials

1 sheet blue construction paper, $8\frac{1}{2} \times 11$ inches
Craft glue or homemade Natural Glue, p. xiv
30 Styrofoam peanuts
20 white cotton balls*
2 very small twigs, 1–2 inches long
2 small black buttons, $\frac{1}{4}$ inch around
1 piece aluminum foil, 5 inches long

*Use unbleached or organic cotton products because fewer chemicals were used to produce them. This reduces the amount of toxic waste.

1. Lay your piece of blue construction paper sideways on a table. This will be the background of your winter scene.

2. Carefully glue down as many Styrofoam peanuts as you want along the bottom portion of your paper to create snowy hills and valleys.

3. Using the glue, draw a snowman shape on the paper and fill it in.

4. Place your cotton balls on top of the glue to create a fluffy snowman.

5. Glue down your small twigs as arms for the snowman. Then put a lot of glue on the back of each button. Put the buttons on top of the cotton balls as eyes for your snowman.

6. Break up your leftover Styrofoam peanuts into small pieces and set aside.

7. Tear up your aluminum foil into small pieces, about the size of the nail of your pinky finger, and set aside.

8. Put glue dots all over your blue construction paper around the snowman figure and up into the sky.

9. Stick your broken Styrofoam pieces and tiny aluminum foil pieces on top of the glue dots. Now you have snow and stars all around your snowman, making a sparkly Winter Scene Art.

When you ship your own packages, think about shredding newspaper to secure items. This can be recycled by the person who receives the package.

Shopping Tote

Ages 7 and up

A cloth bag for shopping or carrying things is something you can reuse all the time. You can take your bag to the store, to school, or to the playground. If you have an old cloth bag at home, you can decorate it and turn it into a piece of art. Stickers, fabric glue (available at craft stores), and permanent or fabric markers will allow you to personalize your bag by sticking on cloth patches, gems, or coloring designs. If you don't already have a Shopping Tote, you can make one from an old pillowcase.

One More Time

Are you wearing some clothing that once belonged to an older brother or sister? What you may call hand-me-down clothing is really a way of reusing something instead of throwing it out. Clothing is just one human-made material that can easily be reused. Baskets are also reusable. Shoppers use baskets to carry their groceries, fruits, and vegetables home from the store. Baskets are also used to give gifts. Materials such as bricks and lumber from old buildings and barns that are torn down can be reused to build new buildings. Old doors can be turned sideways and used as shelves and tables. People are being more creative about products to reuse. Can you find things in your home that you can reuse one more time instead of throwing out?

Adult supervision required

Materials

Pillowcase

Scissors

Strong thread

Sewing needle

Stickers, fabric glue (available at craft stores), and permanent or fabric markers

Cloth patches, gems, or coloring designs

1. The opening of the pillowcase has a 3–4 inch pre-sewn border. Cut this border off and use it as your bag handle.
2. Put the border back around the top of the pillowcase. Fold the ragged edge of the pillowcase over the top of the cut-off border.
3. Thread the needle and sew the border inside the fold (or ask an adult). The border will be floating inside the area you sew but will not be sewn down. It will work like a drawstring on a pair of pants. Once you fold the ragged edge over the border, sew one side of the ragged edge straight across the front of the pillowcase but not all the way to each side. Instead leave a little open on the side so that you can reach up inside to your border.
4. Sew the ragged edge down straight across the back. Again, be sure not to sew through the border but that it floats just inside like a drawstring. Also be sure to leave the border peeking out on each side. Do not sew through the border.
5. Repeat this step by sewing over the top of the same lines you just sewed to make a strong seam.
6. Pull the border loops from the sides. Your bag top will pull together like a drawstring bag.
7. Put your Shopping Tote on a flat surface. Color a design on the front using the markers. Or glue on some gems or stickers to decorate it.

Treat Boxes

Ages 7 and up

Fast-food containers, such as those used for children's meals, Styrofoam and cardboard hamburger holders, and leftover cartons can be reused again and again as Treat Boxes. Remember to always think about how you can creatively reuse products and make less waste. Treat Boxes are a way to reuse products and make your family and friends very happy!

Materials

Dishwashing soap

Water

Dishcloth or towel

Rubber cement

Bag of colored leaves

Other nature items, such as grasses, flowers, and
    pebbles (all optional)

Hole punch

1 piece paper, any kind, 3 × 5 inches

Scissors

Pen or colored marker

Raffia

1. Put a small bit of dishwashing soap on a damp rag or dishtowel.
2. Use hot water to rinse the food container. Then gently wipe out the inside and outside of your container until it is clean. Rinse and let dry.
3. Cover the top with rubber cement. Press down your leaves until you cover it completely, or make your own design.
4. You may also want to add other decorations at this time.
5. Let dry completely.
6. Cover the sides and bottoms with leaves. Let dry.
7. With the hole punch, punch a small hole on the front of the lid.
8. With a pen or marker, copy the following message on the small piece of paper.

> *With my friend I want to share*
> *A special treat because I care.*
> *But keep this box I made with pride*
> *And put a treat of yours inside.*
> *Then pass it on to another friend*
> *In hopes the sharing will never end.*

9. Use scissors to cut around this message, making a neat shape or soft edge. Be sure to leave room for a place to make a hole punch on top (or gently punch through the leaves you've placed in that spot).

10. Thread the piece of raffia through the message. Tie it to the hole punch on the lid. Your Treat Box is ready to fill and give.

Jazzy Jars

Ages 6 and under

Glass containers for gift-giving, storing left-over food or craft materials, or drinking and eating from are much better for the environment. You can reuse them over and over and not have to throw them away.

Materials

Jars and lids

Dishwashing soap

Dishtowel

1 cup water

3 sheets old newspaper

Glass paints (available at craft stores)

2 sheets waxed paper

Small paintbrushes, various sizes

Rag

Rubber cement

1 cup tiny pebbles or shells

1. With dishwashing soap and water, clean out all the jars and dry them well with the dishtowel.
2. Spread the newspapers on a table or workspace.
3. Place the sheets of waxed paper on top of each other on the newspaper.
4. Pour some of the glass paints on the waxed paper.
5. Dip the paintbrush in the paints and decorate the outside part of the glass jars. Keep a rag and a cup of water nearby to clean your paintbrush before using another color. Use the smallest paintbrush for detail work and a larger paintbrush for painting a larger area.
6. Set aside to dry.

7. Now decorate your lids. Cover the tops of the lids with rubber cement and stick on some pebbles and/or shells. Set them aside and let dry completely. When the jars and lids are dry, you can use them to eat, drink, or store things inside. If the Jazzy Jars are large, you can store beans, couscous, or pretzels inside. If they're tall and thin, think about keeping olive oil within. Once you fill them up, you can fill your shelves with earth-friendly art.

Crazy Quilt Boxes

Ages 6 and under

Quilting is a popular practice in America and has become a form of art. One style of quilt is called a *crazy quilt* because it has all types of colors and fabrics, sewn together in no particular pattern. You can make your own form of American art by taking scraps of fabric that might otherwise become waste and turn them into a Crazy Quilt Box that can be used over and over again.

Materials

3 sheets old newspaper

30 or more scraps of fabric cut into small pieces of any size. (This fabric can come from old clothing, socks, towels, sewing materials, or anything that might otherwise be thrown away.)

Scissors

Shoebox

Mod Podge, matte or glossy

Paintbrush, 1 inch wide

3 yards ribbon, 2 inches wide

Cup

1. Spread sheets of newspaper on top of your work surface.
2. Cut or tear all of your fabric into small pieces no bigger than 4 inches wide.
3. Remove the lid of your shoebox and lay it on the newspaper.
4. Take the bottom part of your shoebox and turn it upside down next to the lid.
5. Begin by taking a piece of your fabric. Use a little of the Mod Podge to stick the fabric anywhere on your shoebox. Repeat this step with scraps of your fabric until the box and the top of the lid are completely covered. The size and color of the fabric pieces do not matter, but make sure that the ends overlap a little, so that none of the shoebox is seen. Remember that a crazy quilt doesn't require a pattern, so place the fabric every which way you can. Don't affix any fabric on the sides of the lid. If some fabric overlaps, trim it.
6. Once your box and lid are completely covered, let them dry completely.
7. Trim any fabric that overlaps the edges of the shoebox and lid.
8. Using your shoebox lid as a guide, measure and cut four pieces of ribbon to run along the edges.
9. Use Mod Podge to attach the ribbon to the edges of the shoebox lid to create a nice clean border. Let dry.
10. Put some of the Mod Podge in the cup. Using your paintbrush, cover all of the fabric on the shoebox and lid. Use a very light coat. Don't use a heavy coat, because you want the fabric to be seen clearly. The coating of Mod Podge is only to secure your fabric in place and make your box sturdy.
11. Let the box and lid dry completely, but move them around on your newspaper so that they do not stick to it. Once they are completely dry, you have a great Crazy Quilt Box in which to store your keepsakes, such as a secret diary or a rock collection. It would also be perfectly wrapped present for a friend without buying any wrapping paper!

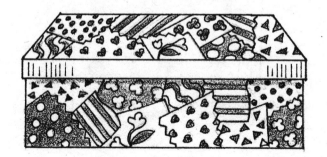

Baggits

Ages 7 and up

Junk mail flyers, newspapers, and old scrap paper will get a new life as a Baggit—an artistic bag you create that can be used to hold a gift or store things in. Instead of wasting wrapping paper, you can give a gift in a Baggit. Best of all, it can be reused all the time.

Materials

1 small paper bag, 8 inches wide and 10 inches high, with twine or paper handles (the kind of bag given at specialty stores for carrying small but heavy items)

Scissors

1 sheet old newspaper

1 sheet colored construction paper, any size, any color

1 sheet colored tissue paper, any size, any color

3–4 colored pieces of junk mail or glossy newspaper ads

Craft glue or homemade Natural Glue, p. xiv

1 small bag

large $1/2$-inch sequin circles (available at craft stores); you can also use buttons or colored construction paper cut into triangles or squares about 1 × 1 inch

12 scraps paper or plastic, 3 × 10 inches (These scraps should come from junk coupons from the mail, plastic top seals from tissue boxes, plastic wrap, leftover tissue paper, or old newspaper torn to this size.)

1 pipe cleaner, any color

4 pieces colored raffia, each about 36 inches long, or colored yarn or ribbon

1. Flatten the bag on your table or workspace.
2. With the scissors, cut up the sheets of newspaper, construction paper, tissue, and junk mail into small pieces about 3 inches in size. Remember that the idea is to make the bag colorful and fun to look at. If you are making a Baggit for a friend, you may want to add picture cutouts from the newspaper of your friend's favorite things—flowers, dogs, or cars.
3. Cover the entire front of the bag with glue. Stick on the 3-inch pieces in all directions so that the front of the bag is covered with scrap paper.
4. Put glue all over the scrap paper now affixed to the bag. Sprinkle a handful of colorful sequins,

buttons, or colored construction paper on the glue. Let dry.

5. While the front of the bag is drying, make your flower bow. Put the 12 3 × 10–inch scraps of paper or plastic on the flat surface, one on top of the other. The pieces should be laid out to look like the spokes of a wheel, each end pointing in a different direction but all of them crossing at the center.

6. Pick up the beginnings of your flower bow. Fold the "spokes" in half, pinching the center so it forms the shape of a flower.

7. Wrap the pipe cleaner around the pinched part and twist it. Leave a few inches of the pipe cleaner as a stem. Carefully separate and arrange the pieces of paper so that they form a flower.

8. When your paper flower bow is complete, drizzle glue on top of it. Then sprinkle sequins or construction paper pieces on top of it. Let dry.

9. Once your bag is dry, flip it over and decorate the other side the same way you decorated the first. Let dry.

10. Take your raffia, yarn, or ribbon. Tie all the pieces around one of the handles so that they dangle loosely all around the bag.

11. Poke the pipe cleaner stem of the flower bow through the top corner of the bag. Wind the remaining wire around the handle.

12. If you like, you can decorate the sides of the bag with more sequins and magazine pictures. Just remember to make sure that all of the glue is dry before you use your Baggit. Give it at least 8 hours.

Broken China Mosaics

Ages 7 and up

Glass is a little more earth-friendly than plastic. Although it is best to reuse and

Art of Recycling

Do you know that plastic soda bottles can be turned into a T-shirt? Amazing things are happening with recycling technology. Recycling can allow manufacturing companies to produce new products or change existing products. One of the best ways you can help to protect the earth is by collecting materials to be recycled into new products. Plastic, aluminum, paper, cardboard, and glass are products that are easy for manufacturers to recycle.

Many households are given recycling bins from the same company that collects the trash. If you do not have an "official" recycling bin, you can create one yourself. Begin by selecting a sturdy container to collect your recyclables. An old trash can or crate (if plastic mesh, reinforce with cardboard) or even a strong garbage bag can be used. Put your recycling bin in a pantry or garage. Make sure that all of the materials you put inside have been thoroughly washed and cleaned; otherwise you may attract unwanted pests.

Ask your parents, teachers, town officials, and local businesses for places where you can drop off your recyclables. Most schools have big bins outside in a parking lot for paper, cardboard, magazines, and newspapers. Schools and grocery stores also recycle bottles, cans, and pop-tops. Sometimes they will even pay you for returning these materials to them! Try to buy groceries and products that come in glass, plastic, aluminum, or paper containers, which are easier to recycle. One way to determine what types of plastic can be recycled is to see if plastic containers are marked on the bottom with a triangle of arrows and a number inside, usually numbers 1 through 7. These numbers are called resin codes and identify the types of materials used to make that piece of plastic. For example, plastics in category 1 include types that contain fizzy drinks. Plastics in category 2 are a little heavier and contain things like milk and dishwashing liquids.

To find out more about types of plastic, resin codes, and how plastic is recycled, check out the following Web links from the National Plastics Council and the National Association of PET Container Resources: www.americanplasticscouncil.org and www.napcor.com/codes.htm.

Don't forget to ask your parents and friends to recycle. If parents or friends don't have recycling bins in their office, school, or home, help them to make one, or let them share yours. A recycling bin is not only a place to gather products for donation. It's also a great source for materials you can use in many of your arts and crafts projects. Aluminum pie plates, bottle caps, plastic bottles, and paper can be reused in all of your organic craft fun! More resources for recycling can be found at www.earth911.org, www.epa.gov/recyclecity, or www.container-recycling.org.

recycle glass, most glass is made from silicates and sand. Silicate is made up of various rocks, minerals, skeletons, and shells of different creatures (in other words, sand). When sand is exposed to extremely high temperatures, it forms into glass. You may remember from chapter 3 how lightning can turn sand into a type of sea glass called a fulgurite. Heating up discarded glass bottles and containers to an extremely high temperature turns them into molten glass. New products can be made from this.

A mosaic is another great way to carefully reuse broken glass. You can also include other broken materials that might normally be thrown away, such as porcelain, clay pottery, and plastic. Instead you can recycle them into something new. When a plate, mug, or piece of pottery is broken, carefully store the broken pieces in a large sealed container. When you have enough to fill the container completely, you have enough materials to make a mosaic. You can collect pretty pebbles or rocks and shells and add them to your materials container to fill it up quicker. To learn more about mosaics, check out *Piece by Piece! Mosaics of the Ancient World* by Michel Avi-Yonah (Minneapolis, MN: Runestone Press, 1993), ages 9–12.

Adult supervision required

Materials

Thick rubber-palmed gardening gloves, or construction gloves
3 sheets old newspaper
Old large platter or dish
Marker or pen
Large container, about 24 ounces, filled with broken china, pebbles, and shells
Mosaic tile adhesive (available at craft stores)
Wooden craft stick
Water

1. Always wear gloves to protect your hands when handling broken china.
2. Spread the newspapers on your table or work surface.

6. Transfer the broken china pieces onto the glue. Hold each piece firmly in its place and count to three. Then spread about 3 inches more of adhesive. Keep adding pieces until the edge of the platter is covered with the pattern of old china.

7. Go back over your finished mosaic, spreading some of the adhesive to cover any sharp edges.

8. Let dry overnight. Your finished Broken China Mosaic can be set in a plate rack and hung on the wall as art. You might want to put a plant in the middle and use it as a centerpiece for a coffee table or for your dining room table or anything else you can imagine!

Recycled Baskets

Ages 7 and up

Don't ever throw a newspaper away. There are just too many craft and art projects that call for newspaper. They can be reused in so many ways to make hats, masks, and gift-wrap. This reuse of newspapers turns the very old art of basket weaving into Recycled Baskets. You can make the same basket out of scraps of fabric instead of newspaper.

3. Turn the old platter or dish upside down and trace around the outside onto the newspaper.

4. Remove the platter or plate. You will be decorating the outer edge of the plate with your mosaic. Practice by arranging the broken china, pebbles, and shells into a pattern on the paper inside the circle. Once you're satisfied with how you've arranged the pieces, it's time to decorate your plate.

5. Using the wooden craft stick, spread some of the mosaic tile adhesive on a section along the edge of your platter about 3 inches wide.

Materials

10 sheets old newspaper

Scissors

Ruler

Heavy-duty needle with a large hole in the top, the
kind used on canvas or other thick fabrics

1 spool twine

1. Cut the newspapers lengthwise into long 4-inch
   wide strips.
2. Tightly roll each strip lengthwise so that you
   have a lot of long, tightly wrapped tubes of paper
   that look like skinny newspaper snakes or ropes.
3. Thread your needle with the twine, leaving a
   long piece of twine hanging from it.
4. Tie a knot in the bottom of the twine.
5. Take one of the tubes of paper and curve it into a
   flat coil that looks like a tight, flat cinnamon bun
   or snail.
6. With your needle and twine, sew the coil in
   place so it stays coiled together and lies flat. Do
   this by poking the needle through the center of
   the coil, wrapping it tightly around the paper,
   and looping it back through to the other side.
   Continue to poke and loop until the coil holds
   together. This is the base of your basket.

7. Now begin to sew on the sides. Put the end of
   another paper tube along the side of the flat coil.
   Sew it firmly in place.
8. Wrap this tube around the coil. Follow with the
   needle and twine, looping it around the paper
   tube and on to the base. Once you have gone
   around the coil once, wrap your paper tube on
   top of itself so that your basket starts to build
   upward.
9. Continue to wrap and
   loop-sew until all of your
   paper tubes have been
   built up into whatever
   basket size you wish. You
   can either paint your
   Recycled Basket or just
   leave it natural.

Egg Art

Ages 6 and under

Another way to recycle food is to create Egg
Art. Perhaps someone is baking a cake and
the recipe only calls for egg whites. Don't let
them throw away the rest of that egg; instead
use it to create dazzling Egg Art. Remember

that *everything* can be reused or recycled. Be sure to use your leftover egg yolk within a day or two so that it doesn't spoil. Your Egg Art can last for several weeks after the egg has been mixed with the other ingredients. But always keep it in an open, dry place, such as pinned on a refrigerator.

Materials

1 leftover eggshell

Cloth napkin

1 piece paper, 8½ × 11 inches

Craft glue or homemade Natural Glue, p. xiv

2 toothpicks

1 egg yolk*

1 paper towel

1 egg carton

Pinch of the following colors: colored spice, such as
    curry or ground mustard, or powdered drink mix,
    or dry powdered paint

1 teaspoon water

1 teaspoon white vinegar

Small paintbrush

*For every additional egg yolk, double the amount of vinegar and water, and then choose another color to add. One yolk should yield one color.

🍃 Nature Notes

Trash Challenge

Here is a fun way to learn and to teach others about how to reuse, reduce, and recycle. Bring your friends, family, or classmates together and challenge them to create less waste with the "Trash Challenge" game. You will need a pencil and paper, rubber gloves, and a trash can filled with trash. You can also make up your own can filled with trash. Divide your group into two teams. Select one person from a team to go first. He or she will put on the rubber gloves and pull out an item from the trash can. If the player's team can find another use for the item, it wins a point. Another use may be an idea for a craft or an art project like the ones in this book. An item can also be used for compost in a garden, as a tool, or as a toy. A person from the other team goes next. Play this game until all the trash is gone. Everyone will have fun learning how to turn trash into treasure! You can set a time limit to make the game more challenging and fun.

1. Clean the inside of your discarded eggshell with water so that no egg white is left inside the shell. Do this by carefully holding the eggshell under a slow stream of water until all the egg white and yolk are washed clean. You can also place your eggshells in a colander and hold it under a gentle stream of water. Let the eggshell dry completely for about 1 hour.

2. Lay your cloth napkin out and put the discarded eggshell in the center.

3. Carefully wrap up the eggshell with the napkin. Then, crush it with your hand. It does not matter how small or similar in size the pieces are. When you open your napkin, you will have the texture for your picture.

4. Put a few drops of the craft glue on your piece of paper.

5. Using a clean toothpick, swirl the glue into any design you wish, maybe a flower.

6. Sprinkle your crushed eggshell onto the glued paper. Let dry completely.

7. While the glue is drying, you can make the color for your picture. Carefully place the egg yolk on the paper towel and gently roll it around until all the egg white is completely removed.

8. Carefully pick up the egg yolk and hold it over one of the egg carton cups.

9. Poke it with a toothpick, and let the yolk drain from the yolk sack into the carton cup.

10. Throw away the yolk sack.

11. Sprinkle on top of the yolk the dry color you have chosen—for example, curry spice.

12. Now add a few drops of water and a drop or two of white vinegar. Mix well with your toothpick. Your egg paint is ready to be used.

13. Dip the paintbrush into your egg paint and add color to the picture on your Egg Art.

Bottle Doll

Ages 7 and up

This little Bottle Doll is a great project to make on a rainy day. She requires some time and hard work, but you will be so happy with what you have made from scraps of fabric and a soda bottle. Your friends will want to make one, too!

Materials

5 sheets old newspaper

1 Styrofoam or newspaper ball, 5 inches across

1 plastic 2-liter pop bottle, empty and washed

Pair of work gloves or heavy-duty gardening gloves

1 strong wire, 18 inches*

Plastic knife

1 Styrofoam ball, 2 inches across

Cookie sheet

Bowl

1 cup flour

3 cups water

Wooden spoon

Shoebox filled with scrap cotton fabric, such as old
   T-shirts, napkins, sheets—anything cotton

Scissors

30 pieces yarn, 6 inches long

Acrylic paints, assorted colors, Nature's Paints, p. 70,
   or Cornstarch Paint, p. xv

1 large plastic lid, such as from a large container of
   margarine

1 cup water

Rag

2 paintbrushes, one about 2 inches wide and the
   other very small

*Be sure to place a small piece of tape on the ends of the wire so
that you won't hurt yourself when you work with it. You can also
use long pipe cleaners, or twist two together to make a long one.
Also try Fun Wire, a wire made for children's hands and available
at most craft stores.

1. Place the sheets of newspaper on the table or
   workspace.

2. Gently set the 5-inch Styrofoam or newspaper
   ball on top of the soda bottle, screwing it on so
   that it stays in place. This is your doll's head.

3. Put on your work gloves or gardening gloves.
   Hold the center of the wire against
   the back of the doll's soda-bottle
   neck.

4. Wrap both ends once around the
   soda-bottle neck, then let them
   extend out in front like arms.

5. Using the plastic knife, cut the
   2-inch Styrofoam ball in half.

6. Put the half-cut Styrofoam ball on
   the end of the wire like a hand.

7. Put the Bottle Doll on the cookie
   sheet on top of the newspapers
   and remove your work gloves or
   gardening gloves.

8. Now it is time to build the body of
   your doll. Make a mixture of
   papier-mâché paste. (Papier-
   mâché paste is easy to make. You
   can use it to create many things
   with recyclables.)

9. Mix 1 cup of flour with 3 cups of water in the bowl. Mix well until most or all of the lumps are gone.

10. Cut fabric with scissors into strips of any size but at least 3 inches wide and 5 inches long.

11. Dip each strip of fabric into the papier-mâché mixture. Gently squeeze the fabric with your hand so that it doesn't drip water.

12. Cover your doll's head and body with the fabric strips. These should be covered completely with a thin layer of the fabric.

13. Wrap the fabric around the wires to make them thicker. Adding multiple layers will do this.

14. When you are happy with the shape of your doll, add hair by dipping the pieces of yarn into the papier-mâché mixture just as you did with the scraps of fabric. You can make short or long hair with the yarn by trimming it as you like. Let dry overnight.

15. When the doll is dry, you are ready to paint a face, hair, and clothing. Use the acrylic paints, cup of water, rag, and plastic lid as a mixing board. Cover your Bottle Doll with colorful paints and any artistic design you would like on her dress.

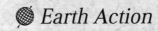 *Earth Action*

Reuse Shoes

Big companies are coming up with exciting ways to reduce, reuse, and recycle. One clever idea is Nike's Reuse-A-Shoe program. Nike is asking local waste companies and schools to collect old athletic shoes for recycling. Nike grinds up the shoes and uses the ground rubber to make sports surfaces. Running tracks, soccer fields, basketball courts, and even playground surfaces can all be made from old, worn-out shoes. Check out how you can turn your athletic shoes into a sports playground at www.nikereuse ashoe.com.

Conclusion

Throughout this book we have learned ways to protect our natural resources. We have learned how to celebrate the beauty of our planet and teach others about our natural environment. But art is just one way to encourage everyone to start thinking about nature. Sharing the process of building and maintaining an earth art toolbox through hikes, walks, and exploration in nature is the most important way to appreciate the art in nature. Sharing the beauty of our earth through your natural arts and crafts will follow from your increased knowledge of the world's natural wonders. As you explore, always try to learn new things about our earth, such as the exciting science behind the creation of sand and rocks, and how trees and soil are important in sustaining our life. Get involved and discover new ways to respect and protect our natural resources. Creating and sharing the wonder of natural art projects is only the beginning. It is up to you to ask questions and to find the answers that will continue to make our earth a beautiful place to live!

Resources for Further Exploration

Here are books and Web sites to help you as you explore and learn about the environment.

Books

Abbott, R. Tucker. *Seashells of the World: A Guide to the Better-Known Species.* New York: Golden Press, 1985.

Armentrout, Patricia. *Read All About Earthly Oddities: Waves and Tides.* Vero Beach, FL: Rourke Press, 1996.

Bartholomew, Alexander, Jill Blake, Brent Elliott, Mike Lawrence, Katherine Panchyk, Denys de Saulles, and Tom Wellsted. *Conservatories, Greenhouses, and Garden Rooms.* New York: Holt, Rinehart and Winston, 1985.

Arnold, Katya, and Sam Swope. *Katya's Book of Mushrooms.* New York: Henry Holt, 1997.

Avi-Yonah, Michel. *Piece by Piece! Mosaics of the Ancient World.* Minneapolis: Runestone Press, 1993.

Bates, Robert L. *Mineral Resources A–Z.* Hillside, NJ: Enslow, 1991.

Blobaum, Cindy. *Geology Rocks! 50 Hands-on Activities to Explore the Earth.* Charlotte, VT: Williamson, 1999.

Brickell, Christopher, and Trevor Cole, eds. *American Horticultural Society Encyclopedia of Plants and Flowers.* New York: DK, 2002.

Coldrey, Jennifer. *Eyewitness Explorers: Shells*. New York: DK, 1998.

Daniel, Jamie, and Veronica Bonar. *Coping with—Paper Trash*. Milwaukee: Gareth Stevens, 1994.

Fischer-Nagel, Heiderose, and Andreas Fischer-Nagel. *Life of the Honeybee*. Minneapolis: Carolrhoda Books, 1986.

Freeman, Marcia S. *What Plant Is This?* Vero Beach, FL: Rourke, 2005.

Hadingham, Evan, and Janet Hadingham. *Garbage! Where It Comes From, Where It Goes*. New York: Simon and Schuster, 1990.

Hecht, Jeff. *Shifting Shores: Rising Seas, Retreating Coastlines*. New York: Scribner, 1900.

Hibbert, Clare. *Life of a Grasshopper*. Chicago: Raintree, 2004.

Horenstein, Sidney S. *Rocks Tell Stories*. Brookfield, CT: Millbrook Press, 1993.

Kendall, Martha E. *John James Audubon: Artist of the Wild*. Brookfield, CT: Millbrook Press, 1993.

Kinser, Charleen. *Outdoor Art for Kids*. Chicago: Follett, 1975.

Kittinger, Jo S. *A Look at Rocks: From Coal to Kimberlite*. New York: Franklin Watts, 1997.

Knapp, Brian J. *Earth Science: Discovering the Secrets of the Earth*. Danbury, CT: Grolier Educational, 2000.

Koebner, Linda. *For Kids Who Love Animals: A Guide to Sharing the Planet*. New York: Berkley Books, 1993.

Laessøe, Thomas, and Gary Lincoff. *Mushrooms*. New York: DK, 2002.

Lember, Barbara Hirsch. *The Shell Book*. Boston: Houghton Mifflin, 1997.

Leuzzi, Linda. *To the Young Environmentalist: Lives Dedicated to Preserving the Natural World*. New York: Franklin Watts, 1997.

Lynette, Rachel. *Caves*. Detroit: KidHaven Press, 2005.

Mass, Wendy. *Stonehenge*. San Diego, CA: Lucent Books, 1998.

National Geographic Picture Atlas of Our World. Washington DC: National Geographic Society, 1990.

Miner, O. Irene Sevrey. *Plants We Know*. Chicago: Childrens Press, 1981.

Palmer, Joy. *Recycling Plastic*. New York: Franklin Watts, 1990.

Parker, Steve. *Waste, Recycling, and Re-Use*. Austin, TX: Raintree Steck-Vaughn, 1998.

Patent, Dorothy Hinshaw. *Feathers*. New York: Cobblehill Books/Dutton, 1992.

Pedersen, Anne. *The Kids' Environment Book: What's Awry and Why.* Santa Fe, NM: John Muir Publications, 1991.

Powell, Jillian. *World Wildlife Fund.* New York: Franklin Watts, 2001.

Rott, Joanna Randolph, and Seli Groves. *How on Earth Do We Recycle Glass?* Brookfield, CT: Millbrook Press, 1992.

Sheehan, Kathryn, and Mary Waidner. *Earth Child: Games, Stories, Activities, Experiments & Ideas About Living Lightly on Planet Earth.* Tulsa, OK: Council Oak Books, 1994.

Star, Fleur. *Plant.* New York: DK, 2005.

Wegen, Ron. *Where Can the Animals Go?* New York: Greenwillow Books, 1978.

Wiggers, Raymond. *Picture Guide to Tree Leaves.* New York: Franklin Watts, 1991.

World Book Encyclopedia. *World Book's Science and Nature Guides: Trees.* Chicago: World Book, 2004.

Web Sites

www.audubon.org. The National Audubon Society's mission is to conserve and restore natural ecosystems, focusing on birds, other wildlife, and their habitats, for the benefit of humanity and the earth's biological diversity.

www.cousteau.org/en. The Cousteau Society is dedicated to the preservation of nature for future generations.

www.earthday.org. Earth Day Network is a driving force steering environmental awareness around the world.

http://eartheasy.com/homepage.htm. Eartheasy offers information, activities, and ideas that help us to live more simply, efficiently, and with less impact on the environment.

www.epa.gov. The Environmental Protection Agency is a branch of the federal government whose mission is to protect human health and the environment. Since 1970, the EPA has been working for a cleaner, healthier environment for the American people.

www.foe.org. Friends of the Earth is the voice of an international network of grassroots groups in 70 countries.

www.fs.fed.us/grasslands/index.shtml. The National Grasslands Visitor Center Web site details the 20 publicly owned nationally recognized grasslands that total almost 4 million acres and are protected by the USDA Forest Service.

www.greenpeace.org/international. Greenpeace is a nonprofit organization that focuses on the most critical worldwide threats to our planet's biodiversity and environment.

www.nature.org. The mission of the Nature Conservancy is to preserve the plants, animals, and natural communities that represent the diversity of life on earth by protecting the lands and waters they need to survive.

www.paleosoc.org. Sponsored by the Paleontological Society, this Web site is a global project focusing on the advancement and research of the study of life in prehistoric times.

www.planetpals.com. Planet Pals at Earthzone is full of fun and facts! Meet Earthman and his Planetpals; they will help you to learn about the universe. Take quizzes, color, play, or make something today! Become a member. Send friends e-mail stickers or greetings. Most of all, be a pal—clean and green!

www.sierraclub.org. The Sierra Club has been instrumental in preserving wilderness, wildlife, and nature's most splendid wild places for more than 100 years. It also helps to protect more than 150 million acres of wilderness and wildlife habitat.

www.un.org/esa/sustdev/agenda21.htm. Sponsored by the United Nations Division for Sustainable Development, this Web site focuses on the conservation and management of environmental resources.

www.worldwildlife.org. Since 1961 the World Wildlife Fund has worked to protect endangered species all over the world.

Teachers' Guide

Activities by Age Level

All the activities in *Organic Crafts* are designed for children aged 3–9, but children aged 6 and under will need some assistance with various crafts. Although these crafts have been developed with very young children in mind, reading the directions, writing, and supervision of the use of glues, adhesives, and scissors is mandatory for this age group. For these younger children, or those who may be challenged by their manual dexterity skills, some craft steps may be completed by an adult ahead of time. This will ease the assembly process and reduce time spent on the project. Alternatively, kids can work on crafts together or as a family, since it is important to promote shared creative and learning time both in the classroom and at home. Always read aloud the lessons and notes that accompany each craft so that children will gain a better understanding of the source of the materials and how our lives have an impact on nature.

Ages 6 and under

Ages 7 and up

All the crafts in this book are recommended for this age group. Many children will be able to read the directions and complete the craft entirely on their own.

The National Science Education Standards

Available through the National Science Teachers Association at **www.nap.edu/html/nses.**

Scientific and educational groups together have developed an approved list of standards for implementation in science education and industry. The National Research Council encourages those working with children in the various disciplines of education and related business and government organizations to recognize the National Science Education Standards as a "vision that provides a first step on a journey of educational reform."

The activities and information in *Organic Crafts* can be used in the classroom to support learning of the following National Science Education Standards:

Science Content Standards for K–4

Content Standard A: Science as Inquiry Standards

1. Abilities necessary to do scientific inquiry
2. Understanding about scientific inquiry

Content Standard B: Physical Science, Life Science, and Earth and Space Science Standards

1. Properties of objects and materials

Content Standard C: Life Science Standards

1. Characteristics of organisms
2. Life cycles of organisms
3. Organisms and environments

Content Standard D: Earth and Space Science Standards

1. Properties of earth materials
3. Changes in earth and sky

Content Standard E: Science and Technology Standards

1. Abilities to distinguish between natural objects and objects made by humans

Content Standard F: Science in Personal and Social Perspectives Standards

3. Types of resources
4. Changes in environments
5. Science and technology in local challenges

Content Standard G: History and Nature of Science Standards

1. Science as a human endeavor

Also available from Chicago Review Press

Insectigations

40 Hands-on Activities to Explore the Insect World
By Cindy Blobaum

This wonderful introduction to insect science for kids age 7 to 10, bursts with more than 40 experiments, art projects, and games—including raising mealworms, using math to measure bug strength, gardening to attract butterflies, and making an amplifier for insect sounds. *Insectigations* provides great playground trivia as well as solid information about the natural world.

Ages 7–10
100 b & w illustrations throughout
$14.95 (CAN $20.95)
ISBN-13: 978-1-55652-568-1
ISBN-10: 1-55652-568-0

Rainy Day Play

Explore, Create, Discover, Pretend
By Nancy F. Castaldo

"Any adult faced with a bored child or, worse yet, a whole roomful of them will find this book a lifesaver." —*School Library Journal*

"Little ones will delight in these creative projects." —*Treasure Valley Family Magazine*

Ages 8 & up
Four-color illustrations throughout
$12.95 (CAN $18.95)
ISBN-13: 978-1-55652-563-6
ISBN-10: 1-55652-563-X

Family Fun Nights

140 Activities the Whole Family Will Enjoy
By Lisa Bany-Winters

Filled with imaginative activities to bring the family together and create lifelong memories, this resource for parents and grandparents is full of activity ideas that require little or no preparation and use materials that are easily found around the house. The 26 themed family events and 140 related activities go beyond game night and movie night by creating family traditions that kids will remember and look forward to repeating. Everything needed to make the night complete is detailed, including skits, songs, crafts, games, and recipes.

Ages 3–9
Illustrations throughout
$14.95 (CAN $20.95)
ISBN-13: 978-1-55652-608-4
ISBN-10: 1-55652-608-3

CHICAGO REVIEW PRESS

Distributed by
Independent Publishers Group
www.ipgbook.com

www.chicagoreviewpress.com

Available at your favorite bookstore or by calling (800) 888-4741